Praise for Positive Reinforcement

"Enhancement of self-concept is arguably the greatest gift a teacher can give to any pupil. The focus of this book chimes with the emphasis on personal development and well-being that runs through the new primary curriculum and OFSTED framework. It provides a multitude of straightforward activities – use them 'straight from the tin' or as a launch-pad for further activities or discussion. There's something for teachers new to the profession and those just looking for new ideas. Use them as starter activities, or main course – or as a 'filler snack' when you feel the need!"

Bridget Knight, Primary Curriculum Network Adviser, QCDA

"Nurturing children's sense of self-worth and confidence in their ability to succeed is undoubtedly one of the most important aspects of teachers' work. It's quite amazing that despite our understanding of the importance of these issues, too many children seem to lose their confidence and self-esteem by the time they are 8! *Positive Reinforcement* should become every teacher's trusted companion. Full of useful activities and practical suggestions, it will be a truly helpful tool-kit for busy teachers who appreciate the value of this kind of work and are willing to give children the support they need and deserve."

Dr Eva Hoffman, Inspired Learning Director Co-founder

"This comprehensive book provides you with a broad selection of activities aimed at creating confident learners by developing pupils' self-image and self-esteem, which helps to achieve the four capacities of the Curriculum for Excellence. Key outcomes of the Health and Wellbeing curriculum are addressed, and as it is the responsibility of all practitioners to meet these outcomes, this is a practical resource for teachers."

Gloria Miller, Manager, John Smith & Son Group Ltd, Jordanhill Campus Bookshop, Glasgow

"In recent years primary school teachers have welcomed the introduction of programmes which develop children's understanding of themselves. It has become apparent that children's emotional intelligence must be nurtured in order for children to learn at their best. Through programmes such as SEAL and Values based Education children are developing a philosophy to understand themselves and their relationships. Peter Clutterbuck has provided a wide range of material in his book *Positive Reinforcement*, for educators to use which will help children not only understand themselves but also teach them how to forge positive relationships with people who they interact with in their everyday lives. The activities are stimulating and can be adapted in an open-ended way to suit the needs of the new primary curriculum. This book is an essential tool for any adult who is working within a 21st century primary school classroom."

Julie Duckworth, Head teacher

"Can there ever have been be a more important time than this to teach about tolerance, empathy, social skills, community values and personal responsibility? This book is easy to read and offers teachers a very accessible set of ideas for helping pupils to develop self-awareness.

"The thought-provoking activities give teachers and pupils useful tools to explore some important social and emotional aspects of learning. Underpinning the activities are the messages that all people are unique and worthy and that self-confidence is borne out of respect for yourself and others.

"Learning how to be reflective is an important part of the approach offered in this book and this, along with an emphasis on gaining control over emotions, resonates well with current ideas about learning dispositions. Recent changes to the primary curriculum suggest teachers will increasingly be encouraged to ensure their lessons promote independence, self-control and self-management and the ability to reflect on learning experiences effectively.

"Above all, the big idea of this book just makes sense. We all know how important real self-confidence is to success. It helps us take risks and persevere, it helps us to be effective problem solvers, to make informed judgements and be self-motivated. Promoting real self-confidence is a good way to promote good life-long learning habits."

Sharon Ginnis, author of *Covering the Curriculum with Stories* and Independent Trainer

Peter Clutterbuck

Positive
Reinforcement

Activities and Strategies for Creating Confident Learners

Foreword by Jackie Beere, OBE

Crown House Publishing Ltd
www.crownhouse.co.uk
www.crownhousepublishing.com

Peter Clutterbuck

Positive
Reinforcement

Activities and
Strategies for Creating
Confident Learners

First published by
Crown House Publishing Ltd
Crown Buildings, Bancyfelin, Carmarthen, Wales, SA33 5ND, UK
www.crownhouse.co.uk
and
Crown House Publishing Company LLC
6 Trowbridge Drive, Suite 5, Bethel, CT 06801, USA
www.crownhousepublishing.com

British Library of Cataloguing-in-Publication Data
A catalogue entry for this book is available
from the British Library.

10-digit ISBN 184590141-X
13-digit ISBN 978-184590141-7

LCCN 2010921504

Printed and bound in the UK by
Cromwell Press Group
Trowbridge, Wiltshire

To Brooke and Jess of Bendingo Bank, Swan Hill

Foreword

'Our children succumb to depression at progressively younger ages and at progressively higher rates.' Seligman 2004.

Can we teach children to be more emotionally resilient and thereby better prepare them for a demanding, ever-changing world where nothing seems completely certain anymore? The SEAL (Social and Emotional Intelligence) programme introduced in the UK in recent years, has shown us that many children benefit from a school ethos which encourages the open discussion of emotions and a curriculum which includes the explicit teaching of the habits of emotional intelligence such as optimism and impulse control. There is much research which shows that many of our young people feel caught between the relentless educational standards agenda and the media frenzy to be cool, rich, thin, famous and beautiful. This book gives teachers an opportunity to focus, not on outcomes, but on reflection in order to develop self-awareness and self-management.

Seligman suggests in his work on developing happiness, that children can be taught to think in ways that will make them more optimistic and thereby more emotionally resilient and indeed healthier and happier. Enhancing self-concept in the classroom through positive reinforcement gives teachers many examples of activities that can help in this crucial process of reflection. If these lessons are delivered as part of a programme where emotional intelligences such as persistence, optimism and self-management are explicitly modelled and taught across the whole curriculum, then students can develop good learning habits which can counter the hedonistic drivers of the 'have it all now' credit card society.

The argument that children should understand themselves as learners and acquire more independence and resilience has been bolstered by some of the latest developments in neuroscience. With the advent of Assessment for Learning, Citizenship and the ECM agenda, the whole composition of the curriculum is suddenly being viewed differently – in a way which puts much greater value on student's ability to think about themselves and their own responsibilities as learners, and thereby as human beings. The skills and competencies needed to develop these responsibilities put the development of emotional intelligence and of wellbeing at the heart of schooling. If implemented effectively, alongside learning how to learn, students will have the chance to develop the tools required to develop the motivation, self-discipline and self-awareness needed to be able to work harder than their teachers, to become successful employees and happier, more responsible citizens. To enhance this ethos, the lessons in this book can also be allied to an active, meaningful student voice programme, intended to encourage a sense of ownership, enterprise and responsibility.

The new primary curriculum gives opportunities for a more flexible pedagogy that will help deliver the confidence for great learning *including* active participation, self-differentiation, choice and challenge that will combine to make learning exciting but demanding. These lessons can provide the ethos that creates a value driven organisation where self-respect and respect for each other facilitate the freedom to love learning. Oliver Adams in his book *Affluenza* discovered that the contagious Western values, which promote materialistic goals, are eroding what really makes us happy – great relationships and feeling valued! Many of the lessons in this book explain and reinforce these essential qualities.

But can we actually teach happiness?

Concerns over parenting skills and the opportunity for ALL children to be nurtured as confident learners are reinforced when we see the huge and growing gap between rich and poor, successful and unsuccessful, achievers and those that disrupt and disdain learning. Schools have more responsibility that ever to ensure that ALL children in their care can learn to value themselves. Teachers have always tried to give students good advice about life, friends, bullying and self-confidence. However, the fact that we have more depression, suicide, self-harm and anxiety in our young population than ever before, means we should warmly welcome resources that give us new approaches and interesting activities to help reinforce a positive self-concept. Despite their fashionable clothes, laptops, i-pods, state of the art mobile phones and flash trainers – children do have to grow up very quickly and live in a world where their own expectations are very high. These lessons provide a philosophy that can grow self-confidence by enabling children to learn to manage friendships and self-esteem.

Carol Dweck has suggested that the most successful learners (those that add most value to your CVA) are those who *don't* necessarily believe they are especially intelligent but who *do* believe that hard work will make them more clever and successful. They know that if they work at it and challenge themselves with tasks they find hard and uncomfortable, then they really can grow their brains. In the classroom, teachers know that achievement can be as much about hard work and self-management as it is about ability. This fits with the core belief that intelligence is learnable, that the harder we work and the more we are willing to try things that we don't find easy the cleverer we can become. This necessitates a resilient disposition, a willingness to try hard, learn from mistakes and take personal responsibility for progress – or lack of it! Such a disposition, alongside excellent communication skills, can and should be explicitly nurtured in our schools. All students want to be popular and to be effective communicators who can express themselves clearly. This is particularly required for many boys, who need practice to get into the habit of expressing their feelings. The high incidence of suicide for young men is a terrifying feature of Western culture. Explicit teaching of communication skills through primary years can help to combat the inability to clearly communicate thoughts and feelings which can lead to introspection and ultimately to depression.

In John Taylor Gatto's account of his time as an award winning teacher in the US, he describes the students produced by our Western education system in this way: 'They hate solitude, are cruel, materialistic, dependent, passive, violent, timid in the face of the unexpected and addicted to distraction.' He recommended 'massive rethinking' to create a more healthy society and a curriculum that doesn't just focus on tests and outcomes but learns by example and reflective practice. Many of the lessons in this book provide opportunities to reflect and build a social awareness that will reinforce community cohesion. When we dedicate time to lessons that enhance self-concept and underpin our curriculum with the values of respect, empathy, friendship and self-awareness, the extra bonus is that we develop not only our students, but our staff and ourselves also. This book provides detailed Teachers Notes that will provide an excellent developmental tool for staff so that they too can reinforce their self-image and be able to model emotionally intelligent behaviour.

Ask any teacher what gift they would like to give students in their care and the answer is always the same: self-confidence. This book is your gift to your students. If you teach it and model it in your relationships with children in your class, you will be giving them the most important gift they will ever receive - self-belief.

**Jackie Beere OBE, Teacher, Trainer and Consultant. Master Practitioner of NLP,
Author of *The Learners Toolkit* published by Crown House Publishing – lessons to help
develop the personal qualities that make successful learners**

References
Carol Dweck, 2000. *Self-theories: Their role in Motivation, Personality and Development* (Psychology Press)
John Taylor Gatto, 2006. *Dumbing Us Down: The Hidden Curriculum of Compulsory Schooling* (New Society Publishers)
Oliver James, 2007. *Affluenza: How to be successful and stay sane* (Vermillion)
2020 vision 2007 Teaching and Learning Review Group (DFES Publications)
Martin Seligman, 2004. *Learned Optimism in Children* (Vintage Books)

Contents

Foreword by Jackie Beere, OBE

Introduction 1

Section I: Learning Who I Am 3
    Spreading the Word 6
    My Learning Diary 8
    Me, Myself 10
    TimeLine of My Life 12
    My Many Names 14
    Some Special Things 16
    Sharing My Life 18
    Guess Who I Am 20
    Knowing Myself 22
    Knowing My Successes 24
    Being Proud 26
    Illustrating My Life 28
    My Own Flag 30
    Sharing My Success Tokens 32
    Positive Handiwork 34
    No Negatives Please 36
    My Self-Image 38
    Evaluating Myself 40
    Positive Feelings 42
    My Positive Jigsaw 44
    Judgement Questioning 46
    Reinforcing My Self-Worth 48
    My Advertisement 50
    Who Am I? 52
    It's OK to be Angry 54
    Where Am I Going? 56
    More Activities and Ideas for Enhancing Self-Worth 58

Section II: Interpersonal Development 61
    Choosing a Friend 64
    Wishing 66
    Connectedness 68
    Our Families 70
    Our Feelings 72
    Bullying 74
    Our Behaviour 76
    Vandalism 78
    Caring for Others 80

Being Positive 82
Self-Esteem 84
Disagreements 86
What Will We Be? 88
Including Others 90
Communicating With Others 92
Managing Our Anger 94
Supporting Others 96
Community Rules 98
Cooperating With Others 100
Winning and Losing 102
Getting On With Others 104
Our Responsibilities 106
Our Community 108
Listening to Others 110
Standing Up for Ourselves 112
Trusting Others 114
More Activities and Ideas for Interpersonal Development 116
The Friendly Classroom 121

Recommended Reading 123

Introduction

Without doubt the notion of positivity illuminates our lives and makes us better able to deal with the stresses and complications of growing to adulthood.

Although teachers generally rate core subject areas such as mathematics, reading and writing as the primary objectives of education many would also readily declare that the development of self-image is high on their list of classroom goals.

This book has been developed to nurture and foster self-image and self-esteem – and provide teachers with a ready list of activities and ideas with which to do so. The activities that follow are based around the assumption that the ultimate right of all students is the right to be oneself.

Positive Reinforcement focuses on developing children's knowledge, understanding and skills in four key social and emotional aspects of learning: empathy, self-awareness, social skills and motivation. It explores feelings in the context of the child as an individual, developing self-awareness and helping the child to realise that it really is 'Good to be me'. The activities help children to understand their feelings and why and how they lead them to behave the way they do – particularly the feelings of being excited, proud, surprised, hopeful, disappointed, worried and anxious. It also explores feelings within the context of children's relationships with their peers, family and friends.

However this book is just a vehicle. The success of the activities and the book's overall influence upon the lives of students is completely dependent upon you as the classroom facilitator and of course your own self-image. Only if you truly value your worth as a human being and feel comfortable about who you are and your right to be yourself will you be able to enrich the lives of your students in this way.

The book is designed for schools who want to build on the SEAL programme for Primary Schools and really focus on *Positive Reinforcement*. It is designed to supplement the Primary SEAL resources and covers a huge range of issues that affect self-esteem and self-worth. Each topic has an introduction and an activity page and full instructions on carrying out the activity. All supplementary materials are supplied on a CDROM for ease of reproduction.

Although the SEAL framework covers self-image and self-esteem, the treatment of these subjects is rather fragmented, running across several of the SEAL Themes. This book covers aspects that are covered in Themes 1, 5 and 6 but it is a focused programme with an emphasis on creating confident learners, confident in themselves and in their ability to learn. This is an essential foundation for their future in secondary school and further education. Building self-worth is not about constant praise for little or no achievement, it being important to find the unique worth in individual children and groups and using that to build positive reinforcement across the whole school.

Part 1 of the book deals with children's self-image and contains lots of activities to build self-worth and self-esteem, to help them perceive themselves as individuals and to help them grapple with how their beliefs and attitudes about themselves form the basis of their self-systems.

Part 2 is concerned with the children's beliefs and attitudes towards others. It is designed to support them in maintaining and managing positive social relationships with their classmates, teachers and others. The development of these positive relationships can bring a sense of belonging as well as the ability to interact and participate in groups whose members are from diverse ethnic and social backgrounds.

The activities in Part 2 are also aimed at enabling children to develop skills and strategies to manage conflict situations in a sensible, fair and effective manner. Through these activities the children will learn the skills to work cooperatively and to balance group commitments with their own needs. Building effective relationships with others has a huge impact on self-confidence and these skills are developed in the same activity-based way. Many of the activities concentrate on building community within the school, concentrating on caring for others, teamwork, etc.

A focus on feelings such as being happy, sad or fearful may potentially give rise to a number of sensitive issues. Teachers need to be conscious of the need to follow the school's child protection procedures if any of the activities prompt responses from the children that give rise to concern. Good communication with parents/carers is a prerequisite to successful work in school on children's social, emotional and behavioural skills. When planning to work on the activities in the book, this becomes more important than ever. The head teacher and the person who coordinates the school's work to develop children's social, emotional and behavioural skills will need to: let parents/carers know, well in advance, that children will be discussing sensitive issues; share the materials that will be used and allow parents/carers an opportunity to raise any issues or concerns they may have; and ask parents/carers to alert the school to any experiences their child has had that might make this area particularly difficult for them – for example, a bereavement.

Positive Reinforcement offers children the opportunity to see themselves as valued individuals within a community, and to contribute to shaping a welcoming, safe and fair learning community for all.

Section I
Learning Who I Am

Me

I am strong I am weak
I am proud I am humble
I am skilful I am clumsy
I am bad I am good
I am sad I am happy
I am sick I am fine
I am smart I am a loser
I am successful I am a failure
No matter what you say about me

I am me

Section I
Learning Who I Am

A positive concept of oneself is not inherited but learnt. As children experience life the impressions they are exposed to shape and influence their self-concepts.

As they accumulate their beliefs and attitudes they interpret any new experiences, to which they are exposed, in the light of these. If any of these new experiences is not considered consistent with their present beliefs and attitudes it may be rejected outright depending on how well the child's self-concept has been developed, reinforced and supported by peers and adults.

Classroom teachers undoubtedly have an important, and often profound, influence on children's self-concept every day. It is the teacher who chooses the influence or effect it will have. If a teacher can help a child with learning difficulties to see him/her self as capable of learning, a naughty or mischievious child as kind, helpful and cooperative, or a doubting child as intelligent, popular or attractive, then that teacher has made a significant difference to the life of that child.

To develop a positive self-image students must experience many successes which then reinforce the beliefs they hold about themselves. These successful experiences will emanate from the safety and encouragement students sense within their classroom.

For this reason class teachers must first of all listen attentively to students and accept their contributions as valuable, and without negative judgement.

The following activities are based around the assumption that the ultimate right of all students is the right to be oneself. It is your right as the child's teacher to be, in all ways, a friend.

SPREADING THE WORD

To ensure students are aware of self-image they must first be made aware of how to accept the encouragement of others.

Once my grandfather and I were visiting a friend who owned a small factory in the suburbs. As my grandfather and his friend, the factory owner, were chatting, a delivery truck pulled up.

"Oh, this will be the boxes of spare parts I have been waiting for," said the owner.

An untidy youth jumped out of the truck and without saying a word began to stack the boxes roughly in a pile near the factory door. When he was finished my grandfather said, "Thank you for doing such a great job of delivering the goods, sir!" The man grunted and said, "You some kind of smart alec, mate?"

"No, I mean what I said," replied granddad. "You did a great job manoeuvring that truck through the narrow lanes to get the goods here safely." "Yeah", replied the man and drove off.

"What was that all about?" asked the factory owner. "People like him never put themselves out. They never do a good job. They don't try at all."

"They're not doing a good job because they feel no one cares if they do or not. Why shouldn't someone say a kind word to them? If we tell people we appreciate their efforts they will do better in the future and they will pass on this new positive attitude to others."

Then granddad winked at me: "Remember, no matter how small it is, no act of kindness ever goes unnoticed."

■ Ask the students to discuss or comment on the grandfather's behaviour. Do you think this behaviour achieved anything? Have you ever offered a word of praise to someone who helped you?

Should we deliberately thank people who provide services for us (e.g. postal workers, taxi-drivers, hairdressers) or are their wages or payment all that is required?

■ Have the students discuss how they feel if someone says something positive to them (e.g. your parents praise you for your progress at school). How might you react to this praise?

Name ....

Date ....

SPREADING THE WORD

It is important for us to reinforce a person's self-esteem by being positive when they have helped us.

In the empty balloons write what you think would be a positive reply to each person.

Here is the meat you ordered.

The taxi fare is £10.50, sir.

I've finished fixing the leaking tap.

I can see you are in a hurry. Get in the queue in front of me.

I have collected your rubbish. The next collection is on Wednesday.

I hope you enjoyed your journey with us. This train terminates in five minutes.

Positive Reinforcement: Activities and Strategies for Creating Confident Learners ISBN 978-1-84590141-7 © 2010 Peter Clutterbuck

MY LEARNING DIARY

Students should be encouraged to keep a diary to provide them with a record of their self-worth.

■ Discuss with students why some people keep an accurate diary of their experiences throughout the day.

Keeping a diary allows you to keep an ongoing record of how you are growing and what is happening to you. It provides a cumulative record of you as a person, who you are, how you see yourself and how others see you.

■ Explain to students that the more you learn about yourself the more you will expand your self-concept and self-understanding.

■ Encourage students to keep a diary or a journal that records their daily thoughts and feelings. In it they can list special things about themselves and the people in their lives.

■ Ask individual students to briefly describe how their feelings and emotions affect their lives. What might they change if it was possible?

■ Ask students to write about the special events of their lives – both good and bad. What effect have these events had on them?

Name . . . .

Date . . . .

MY LEARNING DIARY

An interesting activity is to record our personal thoughts and beliefs in a diary.

Date . . . .

I Have Learned

. . . .

. . . .

. . . .

. . . .

. . . .

. . . .

. . . .

■ In the box write down some things that you have learned about yourself. Record your feelings and desires rather than schoolwork.

■ Now write one or more sentences explaining how you feel right at this moment. Choose words from the boxes below.

angry	happy
sad	tired

upset	worried
timid	glad

proud	kind
grumpy	confident

. . . .

. . . .

. . . .

. . . .

. . . .

. . . .

9

Positive Reinforcement: Activities and Strategies for Creating Confident Learners ISBN 978-1845901141-7 © 2010 Peter Clutterbuck

ME, MYSELF

In order to be prepared to take risks students must first be aware of who they are, where they are and where they are going.

■ Ask students to look up the words *autobiography* and *biography* in a dictionary. Have them tell you what the words mean. Point out the word *autos* is from the language of the ancient Greeks and means "self".

■ Ask students to write an autobiography of their favourite pet (as written by the pet itself).

■ Invite the students to list their heroes from the world of sport or entertainment. Have them choose one and research that person's life. They may wish to produce a fact sheet on that individual.

■ Ask students to consider:
  ● The person who is most influential in their lives today.
  ● When they first began school who did they admire the most?
  ● Who were they really scared of?
  ● Do they still feel the same way about these people?

Name ....

Date ....

ME, MYSELF

How much do you really know about yourself? This activity will help you determine certain information.

Complete this autobiographical questionnaire.

■ Name .... ■ Date of Birth ....

■ Address .... ■ Email ....

■ List five words that best describe you when you first began school.

....

■ List five words that best describe you today.

....

■ How do you spend your time at the weekend or after school?

....

....

■ Of all the things you do in your free time which do you like

the most? ....

the least? ....

■ What was your favourite game or sport when you were 5 years old and what is it today?

....

■ Who is your best friend?

....

■ Has this person always been your best friend? ....

■ What do you find to like about this friend? ....

....

■ What major goals are you working on at the moment?

....

....

....

Positive Reinforcement: Activities and Strategies for Creating Confident Learners ISBN 978-1845901417 © 2010 Peter Clutterbuck

TIMELINE OF MY LIFE

Developing a personal timeline is a great way for students to construct an outline for an autobiography.

■ Begin by asking students to recall and share significant events that have affected their lives to date. These experiences should involve their feelings and attitudes about themselves.

■ Ask the students to illustrate special events that have occurred during their lives – both positive and negative (e.g. starting school, travel, special gifts, illnesses and injuries).

■ Encourage students to compare the special events that have occurred in their lives with each other. Ask them to research how two lives may be very similar.

■ Ask the students to openly and frankly discuss if they are content with their lives so far:
  ● Would you like it to have been better? If so, how?
  ● Would you like help or advice?
  ● What aspirations do you have for the future?
  ● Do you think you will achieve your goals?

Name ....

Date ....

TIMELINE OF MY LIFE

A timeline is a positive way to record and recall significant happenings and events.

On the lines beginning with your birth date write in any significant events in your life. In the space above the writing choose two or three of these events and illustrate them.

Birth   **Today**

Positive Reinforcement: Activities and Strategies for Creating Confident Learners ISBN 978-1845901141-7 © 2010 Peter Clutterbuck

MY MANY NAMES

Names are an important element of self-identification – they tell us who we are and what we represent.

■ Tell the students the following story:

> A teacher once introduced himself to his new class. "I am Mr Jones, but you may call me by my first name."
>
> "What's that?" asked one of the students.
>
> "Mr", replied the teacher.

■ Get the students to sit in a circle and have a short discussion about given names and family names. Explain that many given names have a meaning (e.g. Mary – dearly beloved, Peter – rock).

Explain how some family names originated from occupations (e.g. Smith, Thatcher, Baker, Butcher) or physical characteristics (e.g. Longfellow, Short, Black, White).

■ Now explain that the students are going to introduce one another, e.g. "I'm Mr Smith." The first student on his right says, "I am Sally and this is Mr Smith." This continues around the circle until everyone has introduced themselves and their neighbour.

■ Now the activity continues around once more. This time the student must add something she is good at or likes – "I am netballing Michelle," "I am hamburger Harry" – and so on around the circle.

■ Now conduct a final round of the circle only this time ask each student to add a word that describes how he or she is feeling right at this moment – "I'm jolly Mr Smith," "I'm sad Sally," "I'm tired Peter" and so on.

Name ....

Date ....

MY MANY NAMES

Our names have special significance and meaning. It is important we respect and honour each other's names.

■ What is your full name? Write it here.

....

Given Name   **Middle Name**   **Family Name**

■ Who decided what your given name would be? ....

■ Was there a special reason for being named this? ....

....

■ Do you like your given name? ☐ Y ☐ N

■ If ☐ N what name would you prefer to be called and why? ....

....

■ Have people given you a nickname? If so, what is it? ....

■ Do you like being called by this name? ☐ Y ☐ N If ☐ N what nickname would you prefer? ....

■ Do you ever call other people by their nicknames? Have you asked them if they like to be called by this name? ....

■ If they didn't what would you do? ....

■ In the box below write your name in capital letters. Underneath write a word(s) with each letter that best describe you.

JUDY e.g. **J** (joyful) **U** (utterly brilliant) **D** (dazzling) **Y** (young)

┌──┐
│   │
│   │
│   │
└──┘

....

....

Positive Reinforcement: Activities and Strategies for Creating Confident Learners ISBN 978-1-84590141-7 © 2010 Peter Clutterbuck

SOME SPECIAL THINGS

This is an excellent activity for building a sense of class rapport through an atmosphere of voluntary self-disclosure.

- Have the class pair off and ask the students to conduct a normal conversation for five or ten minutes. Each person must tell the other as much as possible about him/herself (e.g. likes, dislikes, fears, favourite sports, favourite foods, past times).

  Encourage the students to pick those things about themselves which they feel are important to share with an acquaintance. Explain to students that it would be unwise to reveal information that should remain private and confidential.

  When the time is up have students come back together in one large group. Ask each student to introduce his/her partner by stating the partner's name and one or two special things that impressed him/her about that person.

  When all the students have had their turn get the group to discuss their feelings about what it was like to talk to the other person and what it was like to be talked about in the group.

- Emphasise to students that although each of us is a unique individual we may also share the same characteristics, feelings, emotions and so on with others.

Name . . . .

Date . . . .

SOME SPECIAL THINGS

Each of us have special feelings about many things.

In the space below draw your face. Underneath your picture write a few lines telling others about you (e.g. feelings, likes, dislikes, friends).

. . . .

. . . .

. . . .

. . . .

. . . .

. . . .

Positive Reinforcement: Activities and Strategies for Creating Confident Learners ISBN 978-184590141-7 © 2010 Peter Clutterbuck

TEACHER'S NOTES

SHARING MY LIFE

There is no doubt that one of the best ways for a class to develop a feeling of trust and respect is through mutual self-disclosure. For an individual's self-concept to be nurtured and developed that student must be in an environment of support and trust so he/she feels secure enough to take risks.

- Have the students sit in a circle. Explain to them that they will have a specific amount of time to give an autobiographical description of their lives.

  Encourage students to share with their classmates the important experiences that have occurred during their lives, beginning with their first memories of childhood which they consider are significant because they left a strong impression on their personality.

- To get students motivated and to help them overcome any possible inhibitions it is best for the teacher to begin first. This helps to create an environment of reduced risk.

- When each person has had a turn ask the students if they would like to go round again and share things they may have remembered while others were talking. Younger students will most likely want to share memories of past illnesses or physical injuries, holidays or birthdays.

- Ask the students to take the opportunity to point out common links among the group (e.g. "Wow I didn't know Sally, Joanne and Tom all swim for the County," "Bill, did you know Sally was also in a car accident?").

Name . . . .

Date . . . .

SHARING MY LIFE

By sharing our thoughts we can learn much about others.

In the boxes below draw pictures to illustrate the statements in your life.

Something I like a lot	Something I dislike a lot
The best day of my life	The worst day of my life
The most exciting thing I've ever done	The hardest thing I've ever had to do
The happiest moment in my life	The saddest moment in my life

Positive Reinforcement: Activities and Strategies for Creating Confident Learners ISBN 978-184590141-7 © 2010 Peter Clutterbuck

TEACHER'S NOTES

GUESS WHO I AM

This activity helps students to get to know each other in a non-threatening way.

- Discuss with students the importance of knowing and respecting others. To do this successfully you must first know something about the other person apart from their physical characteristics.

- Have each person fill in the questions on the next page. These can be distributed around the room when completed. Classmates read the information and make a guess about who is being described.

- Students should correlate their guesses between the physical characteristics questions and the other part of the questionnaire to see if they have guessed correctly.

- Teachers should also include a form of their own to add interest to this activity.

- Students will only develop a good feeling about themselves when they know other people are interested in them and recognise them as individuals.

- Explain to the students that when we don't know someone we tend to fill in this lack of knowledge with our own assumptions, fantasies and other unrealistic expectations. As we learn more about another and get to know them it leads us to a greater understanding of them and ourselves. Instead of judging others simply by what we see we come to have a deeper appreciation of them as a human being.

A person once said: "*I am someone.* **No matter how poor, or how ill and feeble I may be**, I am someone."

Date . . . .

GUESS WHO I AM

This activity helps us determine how much we know about each other.

The Me You See

My hair colour is	. . . .
My eye colour is	. . . .
My height is	. . . .
My other physical features include	. . . .
WHO AM I?	. . . .

The Me You Don't See

My favourite possession	. . . .
My favourite sport	. . . .
My favourite football team	. . . .
My favourite food	. . . .
My favourite toy	. . . .
What makes me happy	. . . .
What makes me sad	. . . .
Something I like doing at the weekend	. . . .
WHO AM I?	. . . .

Positive Reinforcement: Activities and Strategies for Creating Confident Learners ISBN 978-184590141-7 © 2010 Peter Clutterbuck

KNOWING MYSELF

This activity helps students to evaluate their lives and lets them focus on the things they have experienced and achieved, or even failed to achieve. It is a way of helping them to develop self-concept and to reassess the direction they may be taking in life.

■ Sit the students in a circle, relaxing them so they will be ready and willing to take the risks involved in self-disclosure.

■ Ask them to share their thoughts about certain subjects which you may suggest:

● What is your all-time favourite book? Why does it have special meaning to you?

● What do you like least about our school?

● What would you do to make our school a better place to be?

■ Allow students to question others about their responses. They may agree or disagree.

■ Discuss with students the saying:

"You can disagree without being disagreeable."

Name . . . .

Date . . . .

KNOWING MYSELF

This activity gives you an opportunity to get to know yourself as a person and express your beliefs, feelings and so on in writing. In this way you can contemplate yourself and your life in general.

■ How would your parents have described you when you were very young?

. . . .

■ How would they describe you now?

. . . .

■ What are two things about yourself that you like?

. . . .

. . . .

■ What are two things about yourself that you do not like?

. . . .

. . . .

■ What have you done that you are proud of?

. . . .

■ What, in your opinion, has been your greatest achievement?

. . . .

■ What is the funniest thing that has ever happened to you?

. . . .

■ Have you ever done something that you now regret?

. . . .

■ If you had to be someone else instead of yourself who would you choose to be and why?

. . . .

■ What do you look for most in a friend?

. . . .

■ What qualities do you have that make you a good friend?

. . . .

Positive Reinforcement: Activities and Strategies for Creating Confident Learners ISBN 978-1-84590141-7 © 2010 Peter Clutterbuck

KNOWING MY SUCCESSES

An crucial step in the development of students' self-identity is to encourage them to focus on the positive aspects of themselves. Students must come to realise that to accomplish their full potential they should not dwell on negative past events but rather build on their successes. Note: Explain to students that success can take many forms – it could be winning a prize or simply having a pet, the first time you go swimming or travel on a bus, a train or an airplane.

■ Have the students sit in a circle. Ask them to close their eyes and imagine there is a very large television screen in front of them. Have them think back to before they started school and project a success they had onto the screen.

Ask questions such as:

- Can you remember a success you've had at this time?
- Where did it take place?
- Did you plan it or did it just happen?
- Did you do it alone or with others?
- Did you tell anyone about this success?
- Can you remember how you felt then?
- Can you recreate that feeling in your body now?

Ask the students to open their eyes and share their success experiences with their classmates.

■ Now ask the students to recall successes during the time they have spent at school and up to the present time.

■ Discuss with students what is meant by the saying:

"Success is not permanent. The same is also true of failure."

Name ....

Date ....

KNOWING MY SUCCESSES

Throughout our lives we experience both success and failure: think about the success you've had.

In the boxes draw pictures that illustrate your successes at these times in your life. Remember a success may be something you have achieved or done for the first time.

Two successes before I started school

Two successes since I started school

Positive Reinforcement: Activities and Strategies for Creating Confident Learners ISBN 978-1-84590141-7 © 2010 Peter Clutterbuck

BEING PROUD

Being proud of oneself is inextricably linked to self-concept. Students should be given the opportunity to express pride in something they have accomplished that might have gone unnoticed or unrecognised.

Unfortunately our culture rarely encourages us to actually state, "I am proud that ..." It is never too late to change this attitude and encourage youngsters to feel good about themselves.

Students may be proud of their families, heritage, accomplishments, awards, skills, personal characteristics or anything else in which they may do well.

It is extremely important for youngsters to receive recognition and positive support for what they do or accomplish.

■ Begin by asking each student to make a positive statement about a specific area of behaviour beginning with, "I am proud that I ..."

You may assist each student by saying something that mentions a specific achievement:

● "Mike I would like you to mention the outstanding job you did of refereeing the class netball game."

● "Sally I would like you to mention your very neat handwriting."

● "Tom, I would like you to mention how hard you've been trying to improve your mathematics skills."

Ensure students begin their statement with, "I am proud that ..."

Name . . . .

Date . . . .

BEING PROUD

Being proud of something you have achieved is a powerful way to make you feel good about yourself.

In the boxes below write about experiences that have made you proud.

I am proud that . . . . **My work at school**	**I am proud that** . . . . **How I've earned some money**
I am proud that . . . . **Something I have done for the environment**	**I am proud that** . . . . **How I have helped someone else**
I am proud that . . . . **Something I have done to fight racism**	**I am proud that** . . . . **Something I have done for my parents**

Positive Reinforcement: Activities and Strategies for Creating Confident Learners ISBN 978-184590141-7 © 2010 Peter Clutterbuck

ILLUSTRATING MY LIFE

This activity provides students with an opportunity to reflect upon their lives through artwork. They are asked to contemplate the events that have occurred during their lives and how some of these events may have had a profound influence on the way they now view certain things.

■ Ask the students to get into small groups and in an atmosphere of trust and goodwill they each take turns at self-disclosure about their lives. Encourage students not to dwell too long on trivial negatives of the past but focus on those things that have had a positive influence on their lives.

■ Now have the students express in drawings their thoughts regarding the statements in the boxes on the activity sheet.

■ When the drawings have been completed ask the students to form small groups and share what they have done with their classmates. When they have finished you may wish to display the pictures on the classroom wall for a few days.

■ Ask the students to reflect on what they have illustrated and how it has personal significance for them.

Name ....

Date ....

ILLUSTRATING MY LIFE

One way we can remember important events in our lives is through illustrating them.

Express in a drawing:

■ The most significant event in your life to this day.

■ Your happiest moment in the last year.

■ Your greatest success or achievement during the last five years.

■ Something you are good at.

■ What you would like to be doing when you are 20.

■ Something you could do to make your community a better place.

Positive Reinforcement: Activities and Strategies for Creating Confident Learners ISBN 978-184590141-7 © 2010 Peter Clutterbuck

MY OWN FLAG

This activity allows students to express qualities that are significant and meaningful to them through symbolism.

- Begin this activity with a discussion on flags and banners that represent countries or organisations.

  Display the British flag and the Australian flag and ask the children to discuss the significance of their designs and colours.

- Ensure students come to realise that the designs and symbols of a flag have special significance and meaning to the people of that country:
  - What does the Union Jack consist of?
  - Do you know why the Canadian flag has a maple leaf on it?
  - Why does the flag of the USA contain fifty stars?

- Ask the students to design a personal flag. It should contain symbols (e.g. animals, birds, toys, machines, colours) which are meaningful to them. It may also provide a way of identifying their feelings towards a variety of people and situations (e.g. friendship, school, special moments, careers, life goals, values).

Name ....

Date ....

MY OWN FLAG

Creating a flag that illustrates things that are important and meaningful to you is a good means of discovering things about yourself.

In the outline create a personal flag that contains symbols, colours, objects and so on, that are meaningful to you and to which you can readily identify.

Positive Reinforcement: Activities and Strategies for Creating Confident Learners ISBN 978-1845901417-7 © 2010 Peter Clutterbuck

SHARING MY SUCCESS TOKENS

This activity is designed to provide an opportunity for students to present tokens or symbols of their success to others. When students see that others value their contributions their confidence and self-esteem are nurtured and encouraged. Success tokens and other meaningful objects represent who each student is and what they represent.

- Explain to students that we all have tokens that remind us of our past successes. Sometimes we refer to them as *memorabilia*. They may be photographs, sports trophies, badges, medals, ticket stubs, certificates, newspaper clippings, autographed objects, ribbons and so on. Children may wish to suggest their own objects that are tokens of success.

- Help the students to understand that we save these objects because they remind us of our abilities and competences, our friendships, our experiences, our popularity and our likeability.

- Have students discuss and list a number of success tokens they would like to achieve in the next five, ten and twenty years.

- Ask students to bring to class at least three tangible objects that help them to recall past successes and personal accomplishments.

- As the teacher ensure you also bring objects of your own to school which you should present to begin the discussions:
  - "This golf ball which I have had mounted was the one I used when I came second in the club championships."
  - "This certificate was the one I was awarded for third prize in a colouring competition when I was in Year 3."

- Divide a large sheet of paper into as many sections as there are students. Have each student draw a picture of their favourite possession in their space. Ask each student to explain their drawing.

Name ....

Date ....

SHARING MY SUCCESS TOKENS

When you freely share your accomplishments with others you are able to think about the positive things about yourself.

In the boxes below describe and draw four success tokens you do not presently have but would like to acquire in the future. Examples might be:

■ FA Cup winner's medal.

■ Your artwork displayed in a gallery.

■ Your name as the main actor in a movie.

....	....
....	....

Positive Reinforcement: Activities and Strategies for Creating Confident Learners ISBN 978-184590141-7 © 2010 Peter Clutterbuck

POSITIVE HANDIWORK

This activity enables students to consider the positive characteristics of their classmates. It involves the students looking at one another, seeing the good in them and telling the other person about it. Such activities build feelings of goodwill and friendship and bolster the confidence and self-esteem of all class members.

- Discuss with students how we feel when someone praises our work or compliments us in some way. Ask them to suggest words which would describe their feelings.

  Explain that when you compliment another person you not only make them feel better – it also makes you feel good.

- Tell the students the following story.

  A young girl was serving in a hardware shop when an important customer approached the counter. He had a large order to fill and began reading out the list politely. The girl, although a little flustered and unsure, did her best to fill the order.

  The owner of the shop became impatient as the girl slowly filled the order. She rushed up and pushed the young girl out of the way and said, "Sally I'll take over. You sweep out the backroom."

  The customer was shocked and angry. "I would appreciate you leaving us alone," he snapped at the owner. "This young lady is doing a great job and providing me with excellent service!"

  The owner, her face flushed at the customer's outburst, moved out of the way and allowed the young girl to continue serving.

- Ask the students to consider how the customer has bolstered the young girl's confidence and self-esteem by his positive behaviour.

- On the activity sheet get the students to draw a silhouette of their hand and write in their name. The silhouettes should then be passed around the room. On the silhouette classmates should write positive, character-building statements about the person (e.g. Mike is a great footballer, Sally is always happy and smiling).

- As a variation students could cut out words or pictures from newspapers that represent their personal thoughts about that person. These can be stuck onto the silhouette hand.

Name ....

Date ....

POSITIVE HANDIWORK

Recording positive statements about your classmates helps you to understand them better.

In the box below trace out a silhouette of your partner's hand. Pass these around. Classmates should write something positive on each hand about the person named.

Name ....

Positive Reinforcement: Activities and Strategies for Creating Confident Learners ISBN 978-1845901141-7 © 2010 Peter Clutterbuck

NO NEGATIVES PLEASE

This activity enables students to understand the destructive effects of "put downs" on class-mates. Everyone can recall how their self-esteem and confidence suffered when someone berated, belittled or humiliated them. Unfortunately in our society there are some people who seem to relish this negative behaviour. It is up to teachers to demonstrate and teach students that this behaviour is wrong and counterproductive.

- Discuss with students what is meant when we refer to a "put down". Ask them to consider why some people seem to enjoy putting others down.

- Ask students to look up the meanings of *envy* and *jealousy* in the dictionary. Have them use both words correctly in sentences.

- Encourage the students to discuss how they feel if someone belittles or humiliates them. Provide them with examples:

  Billy: I'm excited that I got nine out of ten right for my spelling.
  Sam: Yeah, I bet the test was made easier for you!

  Joanne: That was a great goal – Sally scored to win the match.
  Michelle: Don't be a loser. A trained monkey could have scored that!

- Have students break up into small groups and role-play people giving put downs. Ask the students to consider what they could have said instead.

- Have students discuss what is meant by the statement:

  "When you use a put down the only person you are really hurting is yourself."

  Ask them if people who use put downs are liked by others.

- Have students make lists of the put downs they hear classmates say at school (e.g. You're really weird, That's a stupid idea, Only boys can do that, That stuff's for losers).

Name ....

Date ....

NO NEGATIVES PLEASE

Thoughtless people often give negative replies which can damage the confidence of friends.

Study what has been said in each speech balloon on the left then write a more positive reply in the balloon on the right.

Can I help you lift those boxes? Don't be stupid – you're a girl	Can I help you lift those boxes?
My family is moving. I wish I could stay here You won't be any loss	My family is moving. I wish I could stay here
Michelle can't seem to understand this maths She's not the brightest light in the street is she?	Michelle can't seem to understand this maths

Positive Reinforcement: Activities and Strategies for Creating Confident Learners ISBN 978-184590141-7 © 2010 Peter Clutterbuck

MY SELF-IMAGE

A person's self-image can determine whether that person is willing to take risks and so achieve to her fullest potential.

■ Ask students to consider this statement:

"The more risks we are willing to take, the more alive we are."

■ Discuss with students what is meant by *self-image*. Explain how we can help others to improve the image they have of themselves by supporting them and giving them encouragement.

■ Ask the students to close their eyes and try to focus on all those things that they feel are good about themselves. Explain how too often we focus on the negative aspects of our lives rather than the positive elements.

■ Discuss with children how they feel about their looks. Write this proverb on the board and ask students to consider what it means:

"Beauty is only skin deep."

■ Ask students to consider what is meant by the term *inner person*. Emphasise that this is more important than someone's physical appearance.

■ Have the students place a large sign at the entrance to the classroom saying

"Today is _____ Day!"

Each day a student puts his name on the poster and is given special privileges. In addition class-mates are encouraged to do all they can to make this student's day a happy and special one.

■ Explain to students that it is perfectly normal for us sometimes to feel unsure about ourselves and wish we were better in some way.

MY SELF-IMAGE

The image you create of yourself fosters your self-esteem and confidence with others.

How do you rate yourself as a good classmate? How do you think others see you? Test yourself by completing this simple questionnaire.

I don't join in many class activities because I think I'll look stupid. ❏ always ❏ sometimes ❏ never	**If the teacher singles me out for something good I have done I feel nervous and don't like it.** ❏ always ❏ sometimes ❏ never
If someone "puts me down" I always try to get revenge. ❏ always ❏ sometimes ❏ never	**If I am asked to thank a visiting speaker or give a talk to the whole class I make an excuse to get out of it.** ❏ always ❏ sometimes ❏ never
When classmates call me names or make my day miserable I make up excuses like being ill to avoid going to school. ❏ always ❏ sometimes ❏ never	**If I see a group of classmates playing in the yard I will go up and join in.** ❏ always ❏ sometimes ❏ never
If we are divided into groups the other students ask me to be their leader. ❏ always ❏ sometimes ❏ never	**To be popular at school I buy the "cool kids" I know special treats so they will like me and invite me to their birthday parties.** ❏ always ❏ sometimes ❏ never

Positive Reinforcement: Activities and Strategies for Creating Confident Learners ISBN 978-184590141-7 © 2010 Peter Clutterbuck

EVALUATING MYSELF

It is essential for students to be able to clarify and verbalise their feelings about themselves in relation to everyday experiences.

■ Discuss with students why it is important that we evaluate the things we do from time to time. We should think about our feelings towards certain issues and people and seriously consider what makes us feel this way towards them.

■ Have students write their own definitions for "feelings" words such as:

happiness   unhappiness   love   hatred   excitement

■ Now ask students to explain verbally what is meant by values such as:

honesty   compassion   courtesy   responsibility   tolerance

Do they feel they practise these values?

■ Discuss ways in which teachers and other adults might evaluate them as people (e.g. their ability to persevere and do better).

How might teachers and adults recognise this evaluation (e.g. school reports, praise, guidance, rewards)?

■ Have students discuss the following statements:

"We exist only because others love and care about us."

"We exist because others think about us, not vice versa."

Ask them to explain what they think they mean.

Name ....

Date ....

EVALUATING MYSELF

It pays to regularly evaluate yourself as a person. Such an activity can give us a feeling of well-being.

Complete the following self-evaluation sheet by ticking the appropriate spaces.

MY PERSONAL EVALUATION RECORD

Evaluation Key

	Good	Satisfactory	Could be better
The courtesy I show towards my teachers and classmates			
The willingness I have to help with classroom chores			
My sense of responsibility towards my own learning			
My willingness to help with tasks and chores at home			
My efforts to help other students and include them in activities			
The fairness I display in games and sports			
The compassion and sense of fair play I have for other students			
My willingness to listen to the problems and concerns of others			
My efforts to eradicate "put downs" from my responses			
My cooperation and desire to learn in class			
My ability to focus on what is good about myself rather than dwelling on negatives			

Positive Reinforcement: Activities and Strategies for Creating Confident Learners ISBN 978-1-84590141-7 © 2010 Peter Clutterbuck

POSITIVE FEELINGS

It is vital that you as a teacher give students every available possibility to develop positive feelings about who they are, what they are and what they want to accomplish.

■ Discuss with students how too many of us feel that we have no strengths and that sometimes we focus on the negatives about ourselves or our lives.

■ Explain to students that we often have a difficult time in accepting our strengths because we think others will feel we are boasting or showing off. To some extent this attitude occurs because there is an emphasis on humility in our culture – it is not deemed proper to talk about your pride, your successes or your strengths. It seems acceptable for people to criticise themselves but not to praise themselves or admit they did well.

■ Conduct a personal "put down groan" session with the children. Allow each child to state loudly "put downs" about themselves (e.g. I am ugly, I am useless at sport, I can't seem to get on with others).

Ensure the exercise is fun and have children groan to be dramatic: "Oooh! I always get my spelling wrong!"

Now ask each child to tell others what their strengths are. Ask them to consider why it is easy to put themselves down yet difficult to say what is good about themselves.

■ A wise person once said:

"Do whatever you do with passion – else don't bother."

Ask students to explain what this person meant.

Name . . . .

Date . . . .

POSITIVE FEELINGS

Being positive helps you feel good about yourself.

It is always good to express how we feel.

Complete each sentence starter in your own words.

■ I feel good when . . . .
. . . .

■ I like myself best when . . . .
. . . .

■ My classmates think I . . . .
. . . .

■ Today I feel . . . .
. . . .

■ Tomorrow I would like to . . . .
. . . .

■ I wish my teacher would . . . .
. . . .

■ I wish my parents would . . . .
. . . .

■ I enjoy reading about . . . .
. . . .

■ I hate it when . . . .
. . . .

■ I think my greatest strength is . . . .
. . . .

■ Some things I can do better than others are . . . .
. . . .

Positive Reinforcement: Activities and Strategies for Creating Confident Learners ISBN 978-1-84590141-7 © 2010 Peter Clutterbuck

MY POSITIVE JIGSAW

The perceptions other people have about you are very important in enhancing your ability to develop as a person.

■ Discuss with students what is meant by the word *friendship*. Is a "mate" and a "friend" the same? Have students list the qualities they feel that a friend should have.

■ Ask the students to discuss the following saying:

"Only a friend can betray you."

■ Tell the students the following story.

> A boy desperately wanted to be a playing member of a local junior football team. However, he was smaller than the other boys and his skills were only so-so. The boy had a strong desire to be a champion like his father had been.
>
> He trained long and hard and eventually to his delight he was selected for the team. On Saturday morning the excited boy was taken to the football ground by his proud father. It would be hard to describe his pride when he ran out onto the pitch with his team mates.
>
> Unfortunately the game did not turn out well for the boy and just before half-time the coach ordered him off the pitch. He did not get an opportunity to play again that day.
>
> After the match, when the disappointed, dejected and lonely boy slipped into the car beside his father he said, "Dad I'm a real loser. I'll never be any good at football. I've let you down."
>
> The father smiled and put his arm affectionately around his son's shoulders and said, "To me son you'll always be a star!"

Discuss this story with the students. Ask them to describe how the boy felt and how the father felt:

● When at last he was selected for the team.
● During his disappointing effort during the match.
● After the match.

■ Give the students the Positive Jigsaw activity page. Have them write their name on it and explain that as the sheets are passed around the room each classmate should add something positive about that person in the space provided (e.g. a good worker, doesn't bother others, always willing to help, fun to be with, laughs a lot).

Name ....

Date ....

MY POSITIVE JIGSAW

Good friends always focus on positive attributes of others.

In each space write a positive statement about the person named. When you have completed yours pass it on to the next person.

Positive Reinforcement: Activities and Strategies for Creating Confident Learners ISBN 978-1845901417 © 2010 Peter Clutterbuck

JUDGEMENT QUESTIONING

It is crucial for students to question their abilities and characteristics in order to assess their own attitudes and behaviours.

■ Conduct a personal yes/no question session with the students. The aim is for students to quiz a partner to see if they can establish their likes, dislikes, fantasies, etc.

At the end of the session they should write one sentence briefly describing the characteristics of their classmate, for example:

● Do you get up early in the morning?

● Do you like a particular sport?

● Do you find school boring?

● Do you have any special interests?

"Michael is an active basketballer who enjoys school."

■ Photocopy and distribute the Judgement Questioning activity sheet. Ask students to think carefully before they answer each question.

Discuss with them how individual questions could give clues to the type of person you think you are or the kind of person others consider you to be.

■ Explain to students that we are three people:

● The person we would like to be.

● The person we think we are to others.

● The person we really are.

Name . . . .

Date . . . .

JUDGEMENT QUESTIONING

Thinking about and providing a reasoned judgement about ourselves and our lives is a sound way to consider how we may improve our performance.

For this activity you must simply read each question, make your own judgement and then tick Yes or No. Then you should complete the sentence stubs below.

Name . . . .

	Yes	No
Do you like school?		
Do you like all your classmates?		
Do you like yourself?		
Do you have fun at school?		
Do you have fun at home?		
Do you have a best friend?		
Do you have lots of friends?		
Are you usually happy?		
Do you like to help others?		
Do you like to play with others?		
Do you like to read?		
Are you a noisy person?		
Are you a selfish person?		
Are you a well-behaved student?		
Do you think you are spoilt by your parent/s?		
Do you always get your own way?		
Do you enjoy learning school subjects?		
Are you a member of any special group or club?		
Do you judge a person only by how they look?		
Do you judge a person by what they say or do?		
Did you like answering these questions?		

■ In a sentence describe the kind of person you think you are.

. . . .

. . . .

■ In a sentence describe the kind of person others think you are.

. . . .

. . . .

Positive Reinforcement: Activities and Strategies for Creating Confident Learners ISBN 978-1-84590141-7 © 2010 Peter Clutterbuck

TEACHER'S NOTES

REINFORCING MY SELF-WORTH

Students must be made aware that they are valued as individuals by their teachers and classmates. Knowing this will encourage youngsters to take risks and gain greater confidence in themselves.

◼ Ask the students to break into groups of four. Make sure they choose students they like and feel comfortable with.

The group must focus on one of their members at a time and tell him all the strengths they see in him. The person focused on is to remain silent. One of the group should act as a recorder and list all the person's strengths. This list can be given to the student at the end of the activity. Remember, only positive attributes can be stated – no "put downs" are allowed.

Before you begin this activity discuss with the class the different kinds of strengths that exist. In this way they will build up a vocabulary of positive reinforcement as you will then brainstorm these words. List these words on the board to remind students during the session.

At the end of this activity have the students discuss how they felt giving or receiving positive feedback. Was it easier for them to give or receive positive statements?

◼ Discuss with students the difference between *judgemental* feedback and *appreciative* feedback.

Judgemental feedback is when the teacher (or adult) is the judge and the student is to be judged (e.g. You did well in your test, You are good at poetry).

Appreciative feedback is when the teacher (or adult or other student) lets the person know they have appreciated or been affected by what they have done or achieved (e.g. I appreciated your hard work, I was very happy with your attitude, I enjoyed your talk a great deal).

◼ Encourage students to use appreciative feedback as much as possible. Have them suggest examples of each.

Name ....

Date ....

REINFORCING MY SELF-WORTH

All of us are worthy people. It is important that we always try to reinforce the self-worth of others.

In the empty balloons write a statement that would reinforce each person's worth.

I am sorry that I played so badly

I guess I just can't get the hang of maths

My parents won't allow me to go on the excursion

I have not been invited to Joanne's party

My mother can't afford to buy me expensive trainers

Have you read the poem I wrote?

Positive Reinforcement: Activities and Strategies for Creating Confident Learners ISBN 978-184590141-7 © 2010 Peter Clutterbuck

MY ADVERTISEMENT

This can be a fun activity in which students are given the opportunity to advertise their strengths, skills and abilities.

■ Discuss with students the reasons why television, newspapers and magazines have advertisements (get them to search through newspapers to view examples):

● What advertisements really make you want to buy the product?

● What advertisements turn you off the product?

■ Have the students suggest words and phrases that are commonly used in advertisements **(e.g. strong, sweet, powerful, economical, beautiful, soft skin, clean breath, chic).**

■ Discuss with students the characteristics that advertisements must have to win their attention (e.g. bright colours, good design).

■ Ask students to think about the role advertisements play in our society and tell them they are going to design a self-enhancing advertisement – it could be for television/radio, a newspaper/ magazine, or be a poster or brochure.

To help those who are reluctant during self-disclosure activities permit two or more students to work together. One may be a good artist, another a good writer or another very creative. Give them several days to develop the ideas to create their final work.

Name . . . .

Date . . . .

MY ADVERTISEMENT

One way we can reinforce our self-worth is through a self-advertising activity.

In the space below design an advertisement that illustrates your strengths, abilities, successes, skills, etc.

Positive Reinforcement: Activities and Strategies for Creating Confident Learners ISBN 978-1845901417 © 2010 Peter Clutterbuck

WHO AM I?

This is an activity to encourage self-disclosure. It assists students in developing a sense of self – their strengths, values, weaknesses, ethnic background and place in the community.

■ Write the words "Who Am I?" on the board. Ask the children to close their eyes and ponder what you have written.

Ask individual students to comment on what these words mean and their significance.

■ Ask the students to write a short paragraph explaining what they think is meant by "Who Am I?" Encourage them to write a few sentences describing who they are.

■ Discuss with students the many physical and behavioural characteristics people may have in common – although each of us is an individual we are in many ways alike.

■ Ask the students to consider the following question:

"If you were to leave this place today how would you best like to be remembered?"

■ Have the students write a make-believe letter that they would like someone to write to them if they left this place today.

Name ....

Date ....

WHO AM I?

This activity now gives you a chance to explore and analyse your personal thoughts and feelings about certain issues.

Complete the following questionnaire in your own words. You can be as open and honest as possible as there is no compulsion to share your answers unless you wish to do so.

■ I like people who ....
....

■ I don't like people who ....
....

■ When I don't like something I have done I ....
....

■ Some day I hope ....
....

■ When I like something I've done I ....
....

■ Something I'd like to tell my teacher is ....
....

■ One thing I really like about my life is ....
....

■ My main goal for this year is ....
....

■ The best thing that could happen to me is ....
....

■ The person I trust most is ....
....

■ I wish my classmates would ....
....

■ Something I would like to be better at is ....
....

■ If I could be really good at something I'd like it to be ....
....

because ....

Positive Reinforcement: Activities and Strategies for Creating Confident Learners ISBN 978-184590141-7 © 2010 Peter Clutterbuck

IT'S OK TO BE ANGRY

It is vital that teachers take time to discuss negative feelings with students. If children assume that feelings of anger, aggression or hate are unnatural or wrong they will begin to see themselves as bad people.

Freely discuss these feelings and provide students with the opportunity to "talk them out" rather than acting them out in a destructive or nasty manner. Students come to understand that feelings of anger are natural and common to everyone, and therefore that it is OK to be their own person.

■ Discuss with students the types of negative feelings we all have from time to time (e.g. hate or anger towards your school, your teacher, your parents, your classmates, your brothers and sisters):

● What might cause them to feel this way?

● When might they begin to feel this way?

■ Ask the students to indicate if they ever:

● Get scared?

● Are afraid of ghosts?

● Get so angry they could hit someone?

● Become afraid when their parents fight?

● Like one brother or sister better than the other?

(Note: Students will only respond honestly if you are able to maintain an open and accepting environment of mutual trust and empathy.)

■ Encourage students to break up into small groups and discuss the questions above. They may create more questions of their own.

When the groups have completed their discussions bring all the students together. Ask if anyone would like to say anything about the questions or describe to the whole class what kinds of things make them angry.

■ Explain to the students that although it is natural to have negative feelings occasionally, we need to be aware that these feelings should be controlled and the energy channelled into other activities (e.g. a person who may feel like hurting someone might take out their frustration on a punching bag in the gym, or an angry person may sit, relax and take a few deep breaths).

Name ....

Date ....

IT'S OK TO BE ANGRY

Becoming angry is a natural and healthy feeling we all experience from time to time.

In each box briefly describe an event that has made you angry, hostile or even aggressive. Draw a picture of the incident that caused your negative feelings to occur.

Positive Reinforcement: Activities and Strategies for Creating Confident Learners ISBN 978-184590141-7 © 2010 Peter Clutterbuck

WHERE AM I GOING?

It is important for children to be given the opportunity to consider their future, including aspects such as goal-setting and becoming aware of the rules for responsible self-growth.

■ Discuss with students the rules for responsible self-growth, for example:

1. *Becoming aware of yourself.* You must consider questions such as: What am I doing? Is what I am doing getting me where I want?

2. *Taking responsibility.* This means you must be willing to accept responsibility for the results of your behaviour. In other words, if you are not getting or achieving what you want it is probably your fault and thus your behaviour must alter.

3. *Looking at the alternatives available to you.* What things do you really *want* to work on and improve?

4. *Developing a plan of action.* Clearly set out the specific steps you will take to achieve your goals.

5. *Evaluating the outcomes.* Once you have implemented your plan of action consider the success you have had. Has it been worth it?

■ Conduct an open self-disclosure session in which you ask students questions such as:

● What would you like to do or have?

● What would you like to do better?

● What more would you like to get out of life?

● Are you doing the best you can at the present time?

● What are you wasting?

● What is too complicated for you?

■ Ask students what is meant by *goal-setting*. Discuss what goals they have set for themselves in life. Let them consider if they feel their goals are realistic. What abilities and qualities will they need to reach the goal they aspire to?

■ Discuss with students what is meant by:

"Those who have too many aspirations will also have too many disappointments."

Name ....

Date ....

WHERE AM I GOING?

During our lives we must make serious attempts to consider the direction in which we are heading.

Study each question below carefully for at least one minute each. Relax your body and mind together. Close your eyes and let go of any emotions you may be feeling at this moment. Now project an image in your mind that answers the question. Draw this image in the box.

Where am I now?	Where am I going?
What obstacles will I encounter?	**What inner quality will I need to be successful?**

Positive Reinforcement: Activities and Strategies for Creating Confident Learners ISBN 978-184590141-7 © 2010 Peter Clutterbuck

More Activities and Ideas for Enhancing Self-Worth

To build a caring, open classroom in which students readily respond to self-disclosure teachers must create a welcoming and non-threatening environment in which all children feel confident enough to take risks.

Here are some activities which help to build an atmosphere of trust in the classroom.

A FEELING OF SELF-WORTH

Ask students to write a paragraph explaining what they could do to make other people feel worthy and valued.

CLASS MURAL

On a long sheet of paper ask the students to work together drawing a class mural which depicts the things they do in common and also some things that are their own.

MY INHERITANCE

Ask the students to imagine they have been left £100,000 by a rich aunt in her will; the only proviso is the money must be given away to deserving people or organisations. Have the students write and describe what they would do with the money.

I CAN IF I TRY

Ask students to create simple, short stories in which they face a test of courage and resourcefulness yet through effort they overcome the obstacles and succeed.

WHAT WOULD I BE AND WHY?

Have students discuss or write their responses to sentence starters such as:

If I were an animal I would want to be a . . . . because . . . .

If I were a bird I would want to be a . . . . because . . . .

If I were a plant I would want to be a . . . . because . . . .

(Have students create as many of their own as they wish.)

GRAFFITI BOARD

Have a large sheet of paper in the classroom on which children can write their own thoughts and ideas. This provides them with a place to let off steam. Replace the old paper with a new sheet every so often.

ME AS A TUTOR

Ask students to share with the class one area in which they feel confident enough to teach another person. This may be a special skill, hobby, sport, musical instrument, special interest, etc. Ask them what they would want to learn if someone in the class had that special skill.

MY EMAIL PAL

Ask the students to write an email describing themselves to a newfound friend. Encourage them to go beyond just physical descriptions by adding details about family, friends, hobbies, favourite subjects and so on.

MY NEGATIVES

Ask students to think about any negative traits they may have and how they might eliminate these (e.g. bad temper, selfishness).

MY POSITIVES

Following on from the activity directly above ask students to think about and describe the positive traits they possess. Have them write a paragraph describing these and how they might use them to better their lives.

SKETCHING

Ask the students to draw a picture of the things they do that make them feel good about themselves.

THE BEST AGE TO BE

Ask the students to write a story titled "The Best Age to Be". Encourage them to state why this would be such a great age. When they have finished ask students to read out their work and have the class discuss each story.

WHAT IT'S LIKE TO BE ME

Ask each child to give a short speech describing "What It's Like to Be Me". It can be humorous or serious. To get the students in the right frame of mind to be enthusiastic the teacher should begin this activity by speaking first on the subject.

Section II
Interpersonal Development

Section II
Interpersonal Development

Section I was directed towards helping students to perceive themselves as individuals and to grapple with how their beliefs and attitudes about themselves form the basis of their self-systems.

Section II is concerned with the students' beliefs and attitudes towards others. It is designed to support them in maintaining and managing positive social relationships with their classmates, teachers and other community workers.

The development of these positive relationships can bring a sense of belonging as well as the ability to interact and participate in groups whose members are from diverse ethnic and social backgrounds.

The activities in this section are also aimed at enabling students to develop skills and strategies to manage conflict situations in a sensible, fair and effective manner. Through these activities the children will learn the skills to work cooperatively and to balance group commitments with their own needs.

CHOOSING A FRIEND

A student's self-image can be improved by having a close friend in whom they can trust and confide. However students must be able to recognise the ways in which real and lasting friendships are made.

■ Discuss with students what we mean when we say someone is a *friend*.

■ Have each student explain what they think the word means, for example:

A friend is . . . .

■ Have students break up into small groups and brainstorm all the qualities they think a friend should have.

■ Have students say who their best friend is and write down why that person is their best friend.

■ Ask students to consider the statement:

"A friend in need is a friend indeed."

■ A soldier once described a true friend as a comrade who would stand in front of you and take the bullet that was meant for you. Would they agree?

■ Ask the students to describe what they think is meant by the term:

"Fair weather friend."

■ Ask students to consider and discuss the following questions:
  ● Can a parent be your friend?
  ● If you are a boy can a girl be a friend?

■ Play the Rolf Harris song "Two Little Boys". Have the children discuss their thoughts about the song's lyrics.

Name . . . .

Date . . . .

CHOOSING A FRIEND

As you do this activity have a think about who your best friends are and what it is about them that makes you like them.

FRIENDLY SENTENCE STARTERS

Complete each of these sentences in your own words.

■ I like my best friend because . . . .
. . . .

■ I like being with people who . . . .
. . . .

■ I like being with people when . . . .
. . . .

■ Cooperation is important because . . . .
. . . .

■ My best friend can be counted on to . . . .
. . . .

■ I can help others most by . . . .
. . . .

■ When someone is really nice to me I . . . .
. . . .

■ One important thing I am learning about being a friend is . . . .
. . . .

■ One thing I like to do with my friend is . . . .
. . . .

■ Two qualities a friend should have are . . . . and
. . . .
because . . . .

■ A person I learn a lot from is . . . .
. . . .

■ The world would be a far better place if . . . .
. . . .

Positive Reinforcement: Activities and Strategies for Creating Confident Learners ISBN 978-184590141-7 © 2010 Peter Clutterbuck

WISHING

Students can use their imagination to make-believe they are anyone or anything they desire. Although sometimes wishes may seem far-fetched and impossible to achieve they are often the child's expression of a real need – such as the universal need to be accepted by one's peers.

■ Tell the students the following story:

> Three friends were marooned on a desert island after their ship had sunk. They were starving and terribly upset at their predicament.
>
> One day one of the men was walking along the beach when he came across a small bottle with a long neck. It was made of copper. He rubbed the side of the bottle to see if it had any writing on it. Suddenly there was a great cloud of smoke and a magic genie appeared.
>
> "Why did you wake me from my sleep?" asked the genie. The man sadly explained the predicament the three were in.
>
> "Well, I'll grant each of you one wish," said the genie but the wish you choose must be wise.
>
> The first man said, "Oh wonderful genie, I would like to be back home." Whoosh! The man disappeared.
>
> The next man said, "Oh wonderful genie, I would also like to be back home." And whoosh, the second man disappeared.
>
> Now said the genie to the last man, "What is your wish?"
>
> The man said, "I'm lonely. Gee, I wish my friends were back here with me!"

■ Make-believe genies and fairies often grant people three wishes. Have the students write the three things they would wish for.

Now ask the students to break up into small groups and share their wishes. Has anyone made the same wishes as another?

■ Ask the students if they have ever wished they could be someone else. Who? Why? Do you think anyone might wish to be you? Why would that person want to be you?

■ Ask the students to consider if they could relive their lives what would they wish to have been different and what to have been the same.

Name ....

Date ....

WISHING

Wishing is something we all do. When you cut your birthday cake what do you wish for? A new computer game, to do better at school, to travel to the moon?

Although our wishes may be sometimes far-fetched and impossible wishing is a healthy and fun thing to do.

Suppose the people in the pictures each had two wishes. What wishes might they make?

Write your answers in this chart.

	Wish 1	Wish 2
Farmer		
Footballer		
Homeless boy		
Old person		
Motorist		
Jockey		

Positive Reinforcement: Activities and Strategies for Creating Confident Learners ISBN 978-184590141-7 © 2010 Peter Clutterbuck

CONNECTEDNESS

Connectedness is all about a person's relationships with others. Students must consider who are their friends and family, what they want from other people and what are the personal values they hold closest in their dealings with others.

■ Write the following statement on the board and discuss with students:

"No man is an island."

Emphasise that we achieve our identity through our relationships with other people.

■ As a home activity challenge ask children to research and record their family tree. You may provide them with a copy of the tree design. When completed ask children to share their findings with classmates:

● Did you get any surprises?

● Is there a foreign country connection?

● Who helped you the most?

● Do you have any famous ancestors?

■ Ask students to brainstorm the methods they use to make friends. Challenge them to think of new ones.

■ Ask the students to write a passage answering the following questions:

● What is it that makes you like your friend?

● What is it that makes your friend like you?

■ Have the class line up in two parallel rows quite close together. One student walks between the lines and everyone touches him/her lightly on the hand and says words of praise, affection or encouragement.

Name . . . .

Date . . . .

CONNECTEDNESS

Connectedness is all about your relationships with other people.

Complete each of the following sentence starters in your own words. Think carefully about what you wish to write. There is no compulsion to share your answers.

■ The things I look for in a friend are . . . .
. . . .

■ I make friends by . . . .
. . . .

■ Classmates make me feel good when . . . .
. . . .

■ Classmates make me cross when . . . .
. . . .

■ I like it when somebody says to me . . . .
. . . .

■ People like me because . . . .
. . . .

■ When others tease me I . . . .
. . . .

■ I stop myself interrupting others in class by . . . .
. . . .

■ Someone I'd like to get to know better is . . . .
because . . . .

■ Classmates think I am . . . .
. . . .

■ My parent(s) or carers . . . .
. . . .

■ I don't like people who . . . .
. . . .

■ If I think someone is being bullied I . . . .
. . . .

Positive Reinforcement: Activities and Strategies for Creating Confident Learners ISBN 978-184590141-7 © 2010 Peter Clutterbuck

OUR FAMILIES

It is vital for students to be given the opportunity to explore and accept their feelings about their families.

■ Ask students to describe their feelings about their brothers and sisters. To encourage the children's confidence in being open about this recount some of your own experiences.

■ Have students write a passage describing situations in which their families show kindness and understanding towards one another.

■ Discuss with students the distribution of responsibilities and chores in their families (e.g. Who cuts the lawn? Who cooks the meals? Who makes the decisions about whether you are allowed to go out or not? Who works? Who decides how the household income will be spent?). Students may wish to compare answers.

■ Conduct a discussion with the students about what constitutes a family. Let them brainstorm their ideas:
  ● Is one parent and one child a family?
  ● What is an extended family?

■ Have the students write a passage describing how each member of a family, including them, is unique and different. Ask them to brainstorm ideas about how these differences can contribute to a stronger family.

■ Ask the students to carry out a school survey of family-based questions (like those above) – students can add more of their own. Ask them to compile their findings and record it to be displayed in the classroom.

■ Discuss with students how the concept of family and family roles has changed throughout history. Ask them to research the family during the twentieth century, comparing aristocratic family members with possible roles played by men and women in working families.

Name ....

Date ....

OUR FAMILIES

There are many things that a family must do around their home whether it is a farm in the country or a block of flats in a city. Often the tasks are divided up among family members.

FAMILY TASK SURVEY

Conduct a survey in your school of the tasks or responsibilities of each person in a family. Record your findings as a graph or in some other way. Discuss with your classmates the significance of the findings.

Task or Responsibility	Father Only	Mother Only	Mother and Father Share	Children
Cleaning the car				
Mowing the lawn				
Cooking meals				
Making school lunches				
Washing clothes				
Deciding what is watched on TV				
Where you will go for a holiday				
How much pocket money children get and how often				
What time you go to bed				
Cleaning children's bedrooms				
Buying the groceries				
Cooking breakfast				
Doing the dishes				
Paying the bills				
DIY/repairs around the house				

Positive Reinforcement: Activities and Strategies for Creating Confident Learners ISBN 978-1845901417-7 © 2010 Peter Clutterbuck

OUR FEELINGS

All of us have feelings. Students should come to understand that feelings of happiness, sadness, anger, jealousy and so on are natural and common to us all.

■ Have students brainstorm the different feelings they have (e.g. sadness, happiness). Discuss with them what is meant by *feelings*. Do "feelings" and "emotions" mean the same thing? Is feeling something hot or cold with your hand the same as feeling sad or happy?

■ Ask students to complete sentence stubs such as:

● I feel happy when . . . .

● I feel sad when . . . .

● I feel angry when . . . .

● I feel sorry when . . . .

■ Have children search through newspapers and magazines and cut out pictures that appeal to them. Ask each student to describe how the picture makes them feel (e.g. a picture of a doctor helping a sick child may make them feel glad, a picture of a young person with a flashy new motorbike might make them feel jealous).

■ Have the children discuss how feelings affect their everyday lives. Ask questions to generate discussion, such as:

● Is it all right to feel angry?

● If someone you don't particularly like is punished, does this make you feel happy?

● Can being happy make you a better person?

● Is it OK to cry if you are sad or very happy?

■ Relate stories about events or subjects that make you happy, sad, jealous, angry and so on. By doing this you will encourage students to share their own experiences.

Name . . . .

Date . . . .

OUR FEELINGS

It is natural for us to have feelings. However, sometimes we have to work hard to control our feelings of anger, hatred and jealousy so they do not take control of our lives.

In the boxes below describe something that has made you have the feelings listed. Draw a picture to illustrate the feeling.

Angry	**Happy**
. . . .	. . . .
Sad	**Jealous**
. . . .	. . . .

Positive Reinforcement: Activities and Strategies for Creating Confident Learners ISBN 978-184590141-7 © 2010 Peter Clutterbuck

BULLYING

Bullying can be a huge problem for some students and can affect their lives adversely in many ways. Children must be given the opportunity to discover ways that they as individuals or a class can deal with bullies and their negative effects.

■ Explain to students that bullying is a very negative trait that can have long-term consequences for the victim and the bully.

■ Ensure students are aware that bullying takes many forms (physical threats/attacks and emotional assaults, such as name calling and teasing).

■ Discuss with students the responses they can use towards a bully. An *aggressive* response usually creates more conflict. However an *assertive* response usually resolves the situation. This is characterised by making a firm request for any provocation to stop or ignoring the person and the provocation. If this fails then the assistance of a third person (e.g. classmate, teacher, parent) will be needed.

■ Have the students make a poster using the letters "DOB" which stands for "Don't Obey Bullies". Ask them to colour in and decorate their poster.

■ Ask children to form select groups and role-play how to deal with a bully:
  ● Stay in control of yourself.
  ● Look the bully in the eye firmly but not threateningly.
  ● Stand tall and speak in a firm but not angry voice.
  ● Don't grovel or try to bribe the aggressor.

■ Ask students to comment on the following sayings:

  "He who fights and runs away lives to fight another day."

  "Be careful of those who kneel before you, they may be reaching for the corner of the mat you are standing on."

  "If you don't stand for something you'll fall for anything."

Name . . . .

Date . . . .

BULLYING

Bullies are students who lack understanding of the feelings and well-being of classmates. Their negative behaviour often places others in danger.

■ What do you think might be the names of the two boys in the picture? . . . .
. . . .

■ What has happened? . . . .
. . . .

■ What do you think caused this to happen? . . . .
. . . .

■ What do you think the man might be saying? . . . .
. . . .

■ What might happen next? . . . .
. . . .

■ What advice might you give to both boys? . . . .
. . . .

■ How would you say both boys feel? . . . .
. . . .

■ Is it only boys who bully other boys? . . . .
. . . .

■ Write a "facts chart" listing five ways to deal with a bully . . . .
. . . .
. . . .
. . . .

Positive Reinforcement: Activities and Strategies for Creating Confident Learners ISBN 978-184590141-7 © 2010 Peter Clutterbuck

OUR BEHAVIOUR

Students must have the opportunity to learn that the positive and negative ways we behave can have an enormous effect on the way others view us.

■ Discuss with students what we mean when we say someone is behaving badly:
  ● Why do some children behave badly at school?
  ● Why do some children behave badly at home?
  ● Why do some grown-ups behave badly?

■ Have children brainstorm the incidents of bad behaviour they have seen at school. Ask them to explain what caused them (e.g. attention seeking, showing off, tiredness, boredom).

■ Ask the students to consider the times they may have misbehaved at home or school. What was their reason? What were the consequences? Did they feel sorry later?

■ Ask children why we would behave differently in the following situations. Have them describe the kind of behaviour that would be expected of them in each instance.
  ● In a mosque, synagogue or church.
  ● At a friend's home.
  ● On the football field or netball court.
  ● During fun activities in the evening on a school trip.
  ● On a class excursion to the zoo.
  ● At a friend's birthday party.

■ Have students conduct a brainstorming session on what consequences there should there be for bad behaviour at school, at home and in the community.

Name ....

Date ....

OUR BEHAVIOUR

Are you aware that how you behave affects the way others think of you?

TV TALK SHOW

A television programme asked students about the kind of behaviours that bothered them most. These are the listings they gave.

.... Tells lies ___   .... Is cruel to animals ___

.... Rarely smiles ___   ....Bullies smaller children ___

.... Makes queer noises ___   .... Very moody ___

.................Insults others ___   ....Unfriendly ___

.... Talks constantly ___   .... Bragging ___

.... Stuck up ___   ....Constantly pokes others ___

Now put an **X** beside the behaviours that bother you the most – put the **X** on the left. Now using the line on the right rate each behaviour from 1 to 5, giving a 1 to the behaviour you like the least.

■ You have probably discovered that many different people or groups of people influence what you say, do, think and feel.

■ What is a teacher supposed to be like? Who decides what a teacher will do?

....
....

■ Now consider why people behave the way they do. For example, which behaviour do you expect of the following people?

Policeman ....

Mother ....

Team captain ....

Judge ....

Champion cricketer ....

Positive Reinforcement: Activities and Strategies for Creating Confident Learners ISBN 978-184590141-7 © 2010 Peter Clutterbuck

VANDALISM

Vandalism is of great community concern and students should understand how and why such negative behaviour harms everyone.

◼ Discuss with students what is meant by *vandalism*. Ask them to delve into the history of the word (i.e. the Vandals and Goths of ancient Europe).

"Vandalism is wanton destruction of property and goods for no reason."

◼ Ask students to describe the kinds of vandalism we may witness in the community (e.g. physical damage to buildings and homes, graffiti).

◼ Have children brainstorm the reasons for vandalism:
  ● Do people have the right to destroy the property of others?
  ● How would you feel if someone wrecked your new BMX bike?

◼ Ask children to describe examples of vandalism they have seen in the local community. Who do they think might have done it? Why?

◼ Have students discuss the punishment they would like to see for certain acts of vandalism. Ask students to form small groups to discuss the following points:
  1. Should parents be held responsible if the vandalism is done by a youngster?
  2. Is it only boys who vandalise or can girls be guilty of it also?
  3. Should youngsters be made to repair or pay for the damage they have done?
  4. Should teenagers who vandalise the property of others be held in detention or even imprisoned?

◼ Have students design and decorate an anti-vandalism poster.

Name . . . .

Date . . . .

VANDALISM

The destructive behaviour of vandalism affects everyone in different ways.

Study the picture then answer the questions below.

■ Can you give a possible reason why the boy is acting this way? . . . .
. . . .

■ How do you think the boy might be feeling at this moment? . . . .
. . . .

■ How do you think the girl in the classroom might be feeling at the moment? . . . .
. . . .

■ What might the boy do next? . . . .
. . . .

■ What might be some consequences of this boy's destructive act? . . . .
. . . .

■ Do you think the boy's parents may be liable for the damage? . . . .
. . . .

■ How might the boy's parents feel? . . . .

■ How might the boy's teacher feel? . . . .

■ How might the boy's friend feel? . . . .

Positive Reinforcement: Activities and Strategies for Creating Confident Learners ISBN 978-184590141-7 © 2010 Peter Clutterbuck

CARING FOR OTHERS

It is important that students understand that when we sincerely care for others, others care for us.

■ Discuss with students the different ways we can care for others, such as:
  ● Parents caring for their children.
  ● Teachers caring for their students.
  ● Students caring for each other.

■ Ask the students to write down ways they can demonstrate their care for others, such as:
  ● Volunteer work.
  ● Helping an elderly neighbour tidy up their garden.
  ● Assisting someone who has been injured in an accident.

■ Have students write short sentences beginning with:

I care for . . . .
because . . . .

■ Play the song "He Ain't Heavy, He's My Brother" to the students. Ask them for their thoughts and feelings on the song.

■ Ask students to describe how they have demonstrated their care towards others in some way during the year.

■ Although we place a great emphasis on caring for others, ask students if they take time to care for themselves:

Are you careful not to place yourself in unnecessary danger?

What are some healthy life choices you can make and what are some unhealthy life choices.

Discuss why some things and people are more important to us than others.

Name ....

Date ....

CARING FOR OTHERS

It is essential to show others that we care about them.

In the empty balloons write a reply that shows you care about people.

Our teacher was in a serious car accident yesterday

Mike's parents are going to separate

Sally is feeling sad because her kitten was run over

I've had a severe pain in my arm for several days

I left my lunch on the kitchen table and I don't have any money

Tammy said her elderly neighbour needs a hand cutting her lawn

Positive Reinforcement: Activities and Strategies for Creating Confident Learners ISBN 978-184590141-7 © 2010 Peter Clutterbuck

BEING POSITIVE

Students should learn that people with a positive approach are more successful in all aspects of life. The best system of positive reinforcement is for the teacher to evaluate a student's work and behaviour from the viewpoint of what is good about it.

■ Discuss with children what is meant by *being positive*.

Write the following statements on the board and ask the students to comment.

"Always look on the bright side of life."

"Every cloud has a silver lining."

■ Encourage students to relate stories about themselves or about others in which even though things seemed bad some good eventually came out of it.

■ Tell the children the following story:

During a war a very brave soldier was badly injured by a land mine. He was in hospital for many weeks as the doctors fought to save his life. Eventually, after suffering a great deal of pain and trauma, his body began to mend.

One day the surgeon who operated on the soldier visited him. He had been very impressed with the young soldier's spirit because not once did he complain about the tremendous pain he was suffering.

"I am sorry we had to remove both your legs from the knee down, but I'm afraid there was nothing else we could do."

"That's OK," said the young soldier, smiling. "At least I won't have to worry about cleaning my boots or having holes in my socks ever again."

■ How did the young soldier show he was still positive about life?

■ Discuss with children why it is important for us to be positive about life and about ourselves.

■ Have children write down all the positive things about themselves they can think of, such as:
  ● I laugh a lot.
  ● I'm a good friend to people.
  ● I'm not a fast runner but I try hard.

■ Have children think about how being positive about themselves makes them a better person and a better friend.

Name ....

Date ....

BEING POSITIVE

It is important that we are positive about ourselves and about other people. We must also look for positive effects that may result from unpleasant experiences.

In the empty balloons write a positive result that may have come out of the bad experience.

I came last in the sprint race

....
....
....
....

I dropped Mum's favourite plate and it smashed into little pieces

....
....
....
....

I crashed my bike and wrecked it

....
....
....
....

I missed out on the job at the travel agency

....
....
....
....

Positive Reinforcement: Activities and Strategies for Creating Confident Learners ISBN 978-1-84590141-7 © 2010 Peter Clutterbuck

SELF-ESTEEM

Students must be aware that the secret to success in all areas of life is to have high self-esteem and self-confidence. Teachers must take every opportunity to ensure students come to believe in themselves.

■ Write the following statement on the board and ask students to consider what it means:

"Nothing succeeds like success."

■ Discuss with students the ways we can assist others to develop confidence and self-esteem (e.g. positive compliments, support). Ask the students to think about positive things they can say to others to help them build self-esteem. These could be recorded on personal sheets and displayed.

Sally's Sheet

Sally has a great sense of humour

Sally has a happy nature

Sally always cooperates and helps with chores

■ Play games such as personal noughts and crosses. Draw a grid on the board and write in it the names of students in the class.

Jo	Amira	Sayeed
Sally	Ricky	Judi
Amy	Bruno	Ainslie

Decide who is O and who is X. The two students playing face away from the board. In turn they each choose a position (e.g. middle centre, bottom left, top right). The teacher or another student asks the player a specific question about the person whose name is in that position (e.g. What colour eyes has Robyn got? How many brothers and sisters has Bruno got?). The aim of both players is to get three X or O's in a row.

Have students design "Positive Awards" on pieces of card. Each student writes on it why they feel another student deserves to receive an award (e.g. I'd like to give my positive award to Simon because he is always helping others, I'd like to give my positive award to Joe because he has a happy smile and makes us all feel good).

(N.B. Ensure no child is left out or ignored.)

Name . . . .

Date . . . .

SELF-ESTEEM

Our self-esteem always becomes stronger when we do something and are successful. This is especially so when we take risks.

In the boxes below describe a risk you took which was successful. If it wasn't successful remember you may at least have learnt something from the experience. Draw a picture of the risk you took (e.g. giving a talk to the rest of the class, volunteering for a task, learning a new concept or skill).

Risk I took was	**Risk I took was** . . . .
Risk I took was	**Risk I took was** . . . .
Risk I took was	**Risk I took was** . . . .

Positive Reinforcement: Activities and Strategies for Creating Confident Learners ISBN 978-184590141-7 © 2010 Peter Clutterbuck

DISAGREEMENTS

Like certain other behaviours and characteristics students must come to realise that disagreeing with others is a healthy trait as long as we know the procedures in how to go about disagreeing.

■ Discuss with children the kinds of things that cause disagreements (e.g. at home, at school).

■ Ask them to describe the situations that might cause them to disagree with their parents, brothers and sisters or classmates.

■ Stress that disagreements happen to everyone and that having an argument doesn't necessarily mean the end of a friendship. Explain that in all disagreements both people think they are right. Sometimes the solution to an argument can be found immediately. At other times people need to avoid hurting the other person's feelings too much at the time by walking away to calm down and then trying to resolve it later. Dealing effectively with disagreements protects friendships and reduces bad feelings.

■ Emphasise to students that in any disagreement they should also try to consider how the other person feels. For example, a student may argue with a parent or carer over the cleanliness of their bedroom or the amount of pocket money they are given each week. As parents are responsible for the home and the amount of money that is brought into it, a child must also consider their feelings.

■ Set up a role-play that involves two students who are disagreeing over whose turn it is to do the class recycling, play with the class football, etc. Also have students come up with some ideas about the kinds of arguments that could be used in role-play.

■ After each role-play elicit positive feedback from both students by asking those who watched the performance questions such as:
  ● What did they do well?
  ● What could they have done to make it better?

■ Write the following statement on the board. Ask the children to consider what it means and if it is true:

"You can disagree without being disagreeable."

Name ....

Date ....

DISAGREEMENTS

Disagreeing with others is natural and healthy. However we must always remember that there are certain ways in which we should go about disagreeing.

In the empty balloons write what you might say if you disagree.

I think all girls are lazy	Our class is the best in the school	Country people are smarter than city people
The X Factor is the best show on television	A hippopotamus is the largest animal in the world	Apples are the best fruit of all
You do not get any pocket money because you have not done your job	I never seem to do anything right	Boys always think they're just so great

Positive Reinforcement: Activities and Strategies for Creating Confident Learners ISBN 978-184590141-7 © 2010 Peter Clutterbuck

WHAT WILL WE BE?

Our goals and desires for the future play a crucial part in our lives.

- ■ Discuss with children the need for them one day to decide what occupation they would like to choose.

- ■ Have students brainstorm different occupations and list them.

- ■ Now ask the children to rate the occupations in categories such as:
  - ● The most boring?
  - ● The most interesting?
  - ● The most dangerous?
  - ● The best paid?
  - ● The easiest?

- ■ Have children discuss the qualities that make people suitable for certain occupations.
  - ● What makes a good teacher?
  - ● What makes a good scientist?
  - ● What makes a good pilot?
  - ● What makes a good nurse?

- ■ Tell the students the following story and have them discuss it:

  Will works as a cashier in a supermarket. He enjoys his work but is often bullied by other employees and some play practical jokes on him because he is young.

  One day the deputy manager came through Will's checkout counter on his way home for the day. Will noticed the deputy manager had a number of valuable items in his pockets. It suddenly dawned on Will that he was taking them home without paying for them. In other words he was stealing.
  - ● What should Will do?
  - ● Could Will be in trouble if he didn't report the theft?

- ■ Have students mime the work done in various occupations while their classmates guess the occupation.

- ■ Conduct mock interviews with students as if they are applying for a job.

Name ....

Date ....

WHAT WILL WE BE?

A curriculum vitae (CV) or résumé plays a central part in job seeking. It provides possible employers with a ready reference of your qualifications and suitability for the position.

Name: ....

Address: ....

Telephone/Fax ....

Email ....

The position I am applying for ....

Name of Company ....

My previous position/s ....

My academic qualifications ....
    (please list schools and   ....
    universities attended)

Special Interests

My hobbies ....

My sporting successes ....

My present community involvement ....

My past accomplishments ....

My personal strengths ....

Skills I possess ....

My reasons for applying for this position ....
....
....

Date: ....Signed: ....

Positive Reinforcement: Activities and Strategies for Creating Confident Learners ISBN 978-184590141-7 © 2010 Peter Clutterbuck

INCLUDING OTHERS

It is essential that students learn the importance of inclusion. This means being included and being willing to include others despite their differences.

- Discuss with students the significance of making all classmates feel valuable and wanted by including them in games and other activities.

- Ask students to describe their feelings when they are included in a game. How do they feel when they are excluded by others from games?

- Read the following story to the students and have them discuss it:

   Shelley was very excited when she received an invitation to Michelle's birthday party. She couldn't wait for Saturday to come. At last it did and Shelley had a great time. It is so nice to be invited to a birthday party by the "coolest" girl at school.

   During the evening Jane asked Shelley if she was "sleeping over". She hesitantly said no. She began to feel a lump in her throat as she realised the other girls present were trying to keep the slumber party a secret.

   She felt really embarrassed when her mother arrived to pick her up and take her home. She knew then that she was the only one not staying. As she slowly walked down the path towards the car, she could hear the shrieks of laughter as the other girls were pulling out their sleeping bags.

   - How do you think Shelley felt?
   - Why do people sometimes leave others out of their activities?
   - What are some possible reasons that Shelley was left out?
   - What might Shelley say when she saw the girls again?

- Have the students discuss the reasons why some children may be excluded by others (e.g. rough play, anti-social behaviour).

- Ask students to brainstorm different ways to welcome a new student to the school.

- Ask students to consider whether a person living in a crowded city could be lonely. Is this possible? Why?

Name ....

Date ....

INCLUDING OTHERS

Inclusion is being included and being willing to include others despite our differences.

◼ Why do you think one of the children is crying? ....
....

◼ Why are three of the children happy? ....
....

◼ What might you say to the unhappy person? What advice would you give her? .....
....
....

◼ What might you say to the others? What advice would you give them? ....
....
....

◼ What do you think might happen next? ....
....

◼ Can you think of reasons some children are excluded from games in the playground?
....
....

◼ Have you ever deliberately excluded someone or encouraged others to do so. If "yes" say why you did. ....
....

91

Positive Reinforcement: Activities and Strategies for Creating Confident Learners ISBN 978-184590141-7 © 2010 Peter Clutterbuck

COMMUNICATING WITH OTHERS

Students must have the opportunity to study the ways we communicate and interact with others.

■ Discuss with students what is meant by *communication*.

■ Ask them to brainstorm the many ways we communicate with others (e.g. speech, signs, signals, telephone, television).

■ Have individual children demonstrate how they could show others how they feel (e.g. happy, sad, terrified, angry) without speaking.

■ Challenge students to make up a secret code to pass messages (e.g. each letter is the letter after it in the alphabet).

Code: J xjmm nffu zpv mbufs.

Decoded: I will meet you later.

■ Ask students to come up with ideas as to how they could communicate from the classroom with another student from their class who is:

● At home ill.
● In the next room.
● In the playground.
● In the bag room.

■ Play a game in which students mouth words silently while their classmates guess what they are saying.

■ Ask students to think carefully about the ways we can communicate our feelings and desires in ways other people understand.

■ Have students write a paragraph describing how some forms of communication have changed dramatically over the years (e.g. smoke signals to emails, Morse code to telephones).

Name ....

Date ....

COMMUNICATING WITH OTHERS

Being able to make your feelings, desires and wishes clear to others is a central aspect of our lives.

Read and complete the following activities.

■ You are in a foreign country in which no one speaks English. You have lost your wallet and desperately need money to buy a train ticket to get to your destination. How would you communicate your need to others?

....

....

....

■ You want to get a special message to a friend in the next classroom before lunch in ten minutes. The teacher will not allow you to leave the room. You do not wish any other students to know what the message is. The teacher will allow those who have finished their work to go out to play.

....

....

....

■ Billy is your best friend. You are the captain of the school football team. Billy has worked and trained hard to be in the team. Unfortunately he is just not skilled enough to play in the team and he is too slow. Explain what you could say to Billy about missing the team without hurting his feelings.

....

....

....

■ A new girl comes to your class. She is from overseas and cannot speak English. You would very much like to be friends with her. How could you communicate your feelings to her?

....

....

....

Positive Reinforcement: Activities and Strategies for Creating Confident Learners ISBN 978-1-84590141-7 © 2010 Peter Clutterbuck

TEACHER'S NOTES

MANAGING OUR ANGER

It is important for students to understand that feelings of anger are natural to everyone. To manage their anger they must be given the opportunity to consider the things that make them angry.

■ Discuss with students the kinds of things that make them angry. Do some things that happen to us make us angrier than others?

■ Develop a number of situations. Have children rate them from 1 to 10 on how angry these things make them (from (1) being not very angry at all to (10) extremely angry and enraged).

● Your parents accuse you of something you did not do.

● You lose your pocket money.

● You forget to bring your homework to school.

● All the students in a class are invited to a party except you.

● You see someone being cruel to an animal.

● Your younger brother is threatened by an older, bigger boy.

● You come last in a race at school.

● Your best friend borrows your bicycle and damages it.

■ Read this story to the students:

Jack has just seen his puppy accidentally killed by a speeding car. He was still stunned the next day. He is so hurt he can't even cry. He can't concentrate on his lessons. At home he doesn't really speak to anyone. His sorrow has turned to anger now he has lost his puppy. After a few days Jack's thoughts turn towards the driver of the car. The man was speeding and careless. Perhaps he wanted to kill the puppy.

A few weeks later Jack remarks that his puppy had very little road sense and was always running out at cars. He couldn't train him to stop the habit. Now Jack is angry at himself for failing to train the puppy correctly. He also blames his parents for not helping him train the puppy. He even begins blaming the puppy for being so stupid as to chase cars.

Gradually Jack began to lose his anger.

■ Now have the children list the targets of Jack's anger:

. . . .
. . . .
. . . .
. . . .

● Ask the students to describe who they think is most responsible for the death of the puppy.

■ Ask students to discuss the saying:

"People with clenched fists can't shake hands."

Name . . . .

Date . . . .

MANAGING OUR ANGER

Anger is a natural feeling. However you must never let your anger have a destructive effect on your life and relationships with others.

FOUR THINGS THAT MADE ME ANGRY

In each box describe an event or occurrence that made you angry, then describe what you did or how you reacted. Draw pictures to illustrate your answers.

I got angry when . . . . **What I did**	I got angry when . . . . **What I did** . . . .
I got angry when . . . . **What I did**	**I got angry when** . . . . **What I did** . . . .

Positive Reinforcement: Activities and Strategies for Creating Confident Learners ISBN 978-184590141-7 © 2010 Peter Clutterbuck

SUPPORTING OTHERS

Students should be made aware that many people in their community need support. This help may range from simply helping to build up a classmate's self-esteem through positive comments to doing voluntary work for a charitable organisation in their spare time.

■ Discuss with children why it is important for us to support each other (e.g. classmates, teachers, community members).

■ Have children brainstorm the ways they can support others:

● By being a good listener.

● By being prepared to help in a time of need.

■ Encourage children to share stories of how they have supported a friend, classmate, sibling, parent and so on in the last year.

■ Ask students to describe the ways these people support us:

grandparents parents police paramedics teachers

firefighters older siblings nurses doctors

■ Ask students to illustrate one of the people above in their role of supporting others.

■ Challenge students to name five occupations and list them in order from 1 to 5 indicating their importance to us.

■ Read the following story to the children:

Rasheed's parents wanted him to learn to swim. Rasheed was afraid of the water, but he was too scared to tell his parents.

At the pool Rasheed's classmates jumped straight in but Rasheed was shaking inside and out.

"Scaredy cat!" yelled one of his classmates.

No matter how he tried Rasheed could not make himself jump in. "Why am I so afraid, but the others aren't?" he asked himself.

■ Discuss what you could do to support Rasheed.

Name ....

Date ....

SUPPORTING OTHERS

One of the most rewarding activities in life is to help others.

A teenage boy once wrote a letter to his local newspaper:

Dear Editor,

Our local town must be the most boring in the country. There is never anything for us to do. Can't the government build more things to keep us from being bored?

A reader wrote back the next week with a simple message for the teenager:

Only boring people get bored.

Have you ever thought about helping others in some way instead of sitting around feeling sorry for yourself?

In view of helping or supporting your community what advice could you give this teenager? What suggestions might you give him about how he could help others in his free time.

....

....

....

....

An Australian teenager began an organisation called MaD (which stands for Making a Difference). The aim of his organisation is to help street kids. What do you think his organisation does to help unfortunate youngsters?

....

....

....

....

Positive Reinforcement: Activities and Strategies for Creating Confident Learners ISBN 978-1-84590141-7 © 2010 Peter Clutterbuck

COMMUNITY RULES

Students must come to understand that school and community rules serve everyone. If rules are broken there may be consequences. However, students must also be aware that on certain occasions some rules are wrong and may need to be changed.

■ Discuss with children why it is important for us to obey rules at school, at home and in the street.

■ Have students brainstorm the many rules we should obey. Ask them to consider things such as:
  ● Who makes up the rules?
  ● What purpose does each rule serve?
  ● What might happen if we break one of the rules?

■ Now ask the children to create rules for the following situations:
  ● A class excursion to the zoo.
  ● A class visit to the supermarket.
  ● A class bus trip to view a rural area.

■ Read the following story to the children and have them discuss it:

Jack was always bragging about how daring he was. At school he deliberately broke rules like not running in the corridors and so on, just to show the other kids how smart he was. Jack was unpopular with the other boys because when they played cricket he would break the rules of the game.

One evening after school as Jack and a group of classmates rode their bikes home they passed a factory that had a tall fence around it. A sign said "PRIVATE KEEP OUT". Jack boasted he could climb the fence and steal some apples from a large tree.

The other boys told Jack to obey the sign, but he just laughed at them and told them they were scaredy-cats. To the other boys' horror Jack climbed the fence and got down on the other side. He laughed at the others. He ran across some boards in the yard. Suddenly they snapped and Jack fell into a deep hole. He could not get out.

  ● What rules did Jack break?
  ● What might happen next?
  ● What advice would you give Jack?

Name ....

Date ....

COMMUNITY RULES

Every community in the world has rules by which people must abide. These could be traffic rules, school rules, grammar rules and so on.

Look at each picture below then answer the following question about each one. Write your answers in the lines.

a. Who usually makes up the rules for each activity?

b. Who do you think should make up the rules? Why?

c. What might happen if there were no rules?

d. Which activity needs the most rules and which the least?

a. ....

b. ....

c. ....

d. ....

a. ....

b. ....

c. ....

d. ....

a. ....

b. ....

c. ....

d. ....

a. ....

b. ....

c. ....

d. ....

Positive Reinforcement: Activities and Strategies for Creating Confident Learners ISBN 978-184590141-7 © 2010 Peter Clutterbuck

COOPERATING WITH OTHERS

It is vital that students understand the importance of being a cooperative member of the class in order to be liked and respected.

■ Discuss with students what is meant by *cooperation*. Have them write down its dictionary meaning.

■ Encourage students to explain why it is important for us to cooperate with our parents, teachers, classmates and so on.

■ Ask students to brainstorm the many ways people in their school cooperate with each other.

Have them consider what happens and what might happen if people don't cooperate. For example, the class decides to weed part of the school garden but some students complain and won't help. What should we say to these students?

Tell the students the following story:

> Today is a big day for Class 6E. If they are voted best performance in the District Schools' Drama Festival, the whole class will win a day's excursion to the city to take part in the County Finals.
>
> All the students, except Michael, eagerly await their time to come on stage. He grumbles and complains and says he isn't going to take part. The others say, "You have to because you have an important role." Mike just shrugs and frowns. "I don't care," he sneers.
>
> Soon the children are on the stage. All of them, except Mike, perform well. When it is his turn he just mumbles his lines, then deliberately pushes a classmate.
>
> However, even though Mike has behaved badly their act still wins. The audience claps loudly as the master of ceremonies tells them they have won an excursion to the County Finals.

■ Should Mike be allowed to go to the County Finals? Share your opinion.

ACTIVITY PAGE

COOPERATING WITH OTHERS

If we wish to be included in the games and activities of others we must be prepared to cooperate with our classmates and teachers.

■ For this activity you must work together in groups of three. The idea is for your group to create the best picture of a dinosaur. One member draws the front of the dinosaur, one the middle and the other the rear. When completed share your dinosaur picture with the rest of the class.

Front	Middle	Rear

■ Set up role-plays for the following:

● You want to go to a disco but you know your parents aren't keen. One person plays the child and other two the parents.

● You are desperate to get a classmate to let you take his new computer game home.

In both cases think of good strategies to use. Don't be afraid to introduce humour into each one.

Positive Reinforcement: Activities and Strategies for Creating Confident Learners ISBN 978-184590141-7 © 2010 Peter Clutterbuck

WINNING AND LOSING

It is imperative students understand that the way we act when we win or lose a game determines how others think about us.

- Discuss with students why it is necessary to be able to show you are a good winner and a good loser.

- Ask the children to describe the behaviours that illustrate how a person who has just won a tennis match can show she is a good winner.

- Now ask them to describe the behaviour that illustrates how a person who has just lost a tennis match can show that they are a good loser.

- Explain to students that they need to have two aims when playing a game. The first aim is to win the game because that will make you feel good and enhance your self-esteem. In others words, explain that winning is important. That is precisely why we play games.

- Now explain that the second aim is to ensure you maintain positive relationships with other players and avoid alienating them.

- Now write this statement on the board and have students discuss it:

  "Winning is important, but how you go about winning is the most important."

- Have the children design a poster explaining to others the qualities and characteristics of being a good winner.

- Ask the students to relate their own experiences of when they may have witnessed good sportsmanship or poor sportsmanship.

- It has been said:

  "A winner says: 'How can I solve this problem?'

  A loser is part of the problem."

  Do you agree with this?

Name ....

Date ....

WINNING AND LOSING

When we win we must remember to act in ways which maintain our friendships. When we lose we can feel pretty bad, but showing you can accept defeat gracefully helps you to keep your friendships.

■ Colour red the comment squares that show the person is a good winner. Colour black the comment squares that show the person is a poor loser.

	This is a stupid game to play.
	Gee, you played well and deserved your victory.
	I never want to play with you again.
	Here, you won well so I'll pack up all the gear.
	Congratulations, you are a better player than I am.
	I hate this game and I hate you.
	I'd love to play you again. Would you let me?
	Someone has to lose and it was me today.
	I never win and I bet I never win another match again.
	You had a lot of luck.
	I tried but I just wasn't good enough on the day.
	I give up, I'm no good.
	You think you're smart just because you beat me.

■ Write the following saying on a poster and decorate it:

"Winning is important, but how you go about winning is the most important."

Positive Reinforcement: Activities and Strategies for Creating Confident Learners ISBN 978-1-84590141-7 © 2010 Peter Clutterbuck

GETTING ON WITH OTHERS

Students must understand that to be included in games and be respected by others it is necessary to know how to get on well with other people.

- Discuss with students why it is important to show others you care about them.

- People enjoy being with others who appreciate the nice things about them and give them compliments that are sincere and deserved.

  Have the students brainstorm the things that make other people like us (e.g. being fair in games, giving compliments, being accepting of others).

- Write the following statement on the board and have students comment on it:

  "Good friends look for the good things in others."

  Discuss with students the importance of giving compliments to others. Emphasise that compliments should not just be about appearances or clothes but also given for things people do well, such as positive behaviour.

  Make sure students understand that they should look for things they genuinely like or appreciate in others, then look them directly in the eye, smile and tell them what they like about them.

  Doing this can make a big difference to someone's life. However, also explain to students that they should never give too many compliments or give a compliment that isn't true.

- Explain to students that there are times in our lives when we all need a few kindly words to build our self-esteem. It is important to feel good about yourself and compliments from others can help do this.

Name ....

Date ....

GETTING ON WITH OTHERS

To be capable of building lasting friendships it is essential that we try to understand to behaviour of others.

Here are some brief descriptions of how children act at school or during play.

Read them through and write the names of two children in your class who you feel best fit each description. Don't write more than two names but it is OK just to write one name, or even none if no students match the description.

■ This student always helps other students	■ This student is very quiet ....
■ This student sticks up for us in the playground	■ This student often looks sad and needs cheering up ....
■ This student is really good at sport	■ This student is sometimes too shy to join in games ....
■ This student often says kind things to others	■ This student thinks no one else likes them ....
■ This student never complains	■ This student often plays alone ....
■ This person tries hard and does really good work	■ This student often gets teased by others ....

Positive Reinforcement: Activities and Strategies for Creating Confident Learners ISBN 978-184590141-7 © 2010 Peter Clutterbuck

OUR RESPONSIBLITIES

It is imperative for students to realise that we must all accept certain responsibilities.

■ Discuss with students what is meant by the word *responsibilities*.

Have them describe and list the things that they must be responsible for each day, such as:

● Keeping your room clean.

● Organising yourself for school.

● Catching the school bus.

● Helping a younger brother or sister to walk to school safely.

● Feeding your pet dog.

■ Make a list of jobs to be done around the school. Ask the students to state who is responsible for each one – head teacher, parents, students, caretaker, classroom teacher:

● Who rings the bell?

● Who decides what games we play?

● Who cleans up the classroom?

● Who cuts the lawns?

● Who decides what we have to learn?

● Who decides what class each teacher will take?

Add more of your own and then ask students to compile a graph of the results.

■ Have students discuss and research how their responsibilities at school may differ from students in other countries.

■ Ask students to describe and explain the responsibilities they enjoy and those they don't enjoy.

■ Have them discuss the consequences of not fulfilling their responsibilities.

■ Ask students to write and describe the different responsibilities these people have at school: parent, teacher, principal and student.

Name ....

Date ....

OUR RESPONSIBLITIES

We must all accept responsibilities at school and at home.

Put a tick in the box that best describes how you feel about doing each thing.

AT HOME

	I really hate it	It's OK sometimes	I always enjoy it
Cleaning up my bedroom			
Doing homework			
Helping with the dishes			
Mowing the lawn			
Minding a younger brother or sister			
Helping to get meals			
Running errands			
Cleaning out the shed			
Making my bed			
Getting ready for school			

AT SCHOOL

	I really hate it	It's OK sometimes	I always enjoy it
Picking up litter in the schoolyard			
Learning Maths, English, Science, etc			
Having library lessons			
Going to assemblies			
Playing sport			
Emptying bins			
Helping to clean the classroom			
Running errands for the teacher			
Tidying up my desk or table			
Wiping the board clean			
Helping other students			

Positive Reinforcement: Activities and Strategies for Creating Confident Learners ISBN 978-184590141-7 © 2010 Peter Clutterbuck

OUR COMMUNITY

It is important for teachers to help students to develop a sense of belonging and identity within their community.

■ Discuss with children what is meant by the word *community*. Challenge them to write their own definition of the word.

■ Have the children consider issues such as:
  ● Are all communities the same?
  ● Are all communities happy?

■ Ask students to draw a map of what they consider to be their community.

■ Now ask children questions to create comparisons between their community and a community in a foreign country, such as Africa:
  ● Do all communities have supermarkets?
  ● Do all communities have cars and buses?
  ● Do all communities have the same rules?

■ Ask students to investigate whether all communities in other countries have lots of schools for educating children. Apart from schools, how might the children learn about their culture?

■ Apart from teachers, who teaches them about their community?

■ Ask the students to describe five things they think are good about their community and five things they think are not so good.

Name . . . .

Date . . . .

OUR COMMUNITY

A sense of belonging to a community helps us to identify who we are, what we are and where we are heading.

All the following sentence starters relate to your feelings about your local community. Complete each sentence in your own words. There are no right or wrong answers but think carefully.

■ I think of our community as being . . . .
. . . .

■ What I like about our community is . . . .
. . . .

■ What I sometimes don't like about our community is . . . .
. . . .

■ There are about . . . . people in our community

■ The people in our community are . . . .
. . . .

■ The services in our community are . . . .
. . . .

■ I help others in our community by . . . .
. . . .

■ Most people in our community . . . .
. . . .

■ In our community you can . . . .
. . . .

■ In our community you can't . . . .
. . . .

■ Each week in our community you can . . . .
. . . .

Positive Reinforcement: Activities and Strategies for Creating Confident Learners ISBN 978-184590141-7 © 2010 Peter Clutterbuck

LISTENING TO OTHERS

It is essential that students are taught the skills and protocols of listening to others.

- ■ Discuss with students why it is important for us to listen to others – our friends, family, teachers and others in the community.

  Ask students to describe what happened, or may have happened, when someone didn't listen in the following scenarios:
  - In the classroom.
  - When crossing the road.
  - When the head teacher was speaking during assembly.
  - On a building site.

- ■ Ask students to brainstorm then create fact sheets about being a good listener, for example explaining how to:
  - Tune in, don't interrupt.
  - Pay attention to what is being said.
  - Ask good questions based on what has been said.

- ■ Have students describe times when they or a friend has missed out on something good because they were not listening (e.g. the canteen manager tells the children that ice creams are free today because it is nearly the holidays and they won't keep for four weeks).

- ■ Ask selected students to role-play mouthing words or short sentences and challenge the others to guess what has been said.

- ■ A teacher I once knew used to yell loudly "I want pandemonium!" when the class became noisy. The class always immediately became quiet. Do you think the students were really listening? Try it out.

- ■ Ask children to take it in turns to give a speech for two minutes. It can be on any topic of interest. At the end of the talk the person speaking asks questions of the audience to see if they were listening to what he/she said.

Name . . . .

Date . . . .

LISTENING TO OTHERS

To be a valued friend you must know the skills of good listening and use them well.

In the balloons write a reply that demonstrates you have listened carefully.

Which would you prefer for lunch – a salad, a tuna sandwich or a pizza?

In what countries are these cities – London, New York, Montreal and Shanghai?

Can you tell me the names of four children in your class who have black hair?

I am not feeling very well. I have a painful ache in my tummy

Positive Reinforcement: Activities and Strategies for Creating Confident Learners ISBN 978-1845901417 © 2010 Peter Clutterbuck

STANDING UP FOR OURSELVES

Students must be made aware that to cope with daily interactions with others there will be times when it will be necessary for them to take a stand on things they strongly believe in.

■ Discuss with students how from time to time we may need to take a stand on certain issues or stand up for ourselves.

■ Ask the students to describe what they think is meant by the word *assertiveness*. Have them share stories in which someone else was being assertive.

■ Write the following statement on the board and have students discuss its meaning:

"If you don't stand for something you will fall for anything."

■ Ask students to brainstorm all the things they could do if someone kept pestering or teasing them. Have them make a class chart on which they list their findings.

■ Set up a role-play in which one student teases another. Teach the teased student how to completely ignore the teaser. Explain to students that if you react angrily to teasing then you are playing right into the teaser's hands.

■ Have students make up humorous sayings to counter bullies or teasers:
  ● "I think you should leave them because the keeper tells us your cage has been cleaned out."
  ● "Don't worry. I'm sure your spaceship will land and take you back to your planet soon."

■ Explain to students that if someone continues to give them a hard time they should seek the help of a teacher or other adult. Impress on all students the acronym DOB – "Don't Obey Bullies".

■ Conduct a class discussion on how you can recognise a bully. Encourage students to be alert to it in the playground, the classroom and after school.

Name ....

Date ....

STANDING UP FOR OURSELVES

Sometimes it pays to stand up for yourself or for your beliefs when it is something you feel strongly about.

How do you rate in standing up for yourself in each of these?

If the teacher punishes me for something I didn't do I will tell him or her that he/she is wrong. ❏ always ❏ sometimes ❏ never	**If a bigger classmate pushes me out of the canteen line I immediately push him/her out of the line.** ❏ always ❏ sometimes ❏ never
When a bigger student teases me or threatens me I tell a teacher. ❏ always ❏ sometimes ❏ never	**If the head teacher tells me something I know is wrong I will tell him/her.** ❏ always ❏ sometimes ❏ never
If a bigger student takes my property I demand it back. ❏ always ❏ sometimes ❏ never	**If I see a younger student being teased or bullied I step in to help.** ❏ always ❏ sometimes ❏ never
If a stranger demands I give him/her money I tell him/her to get lost. ❏ always ❏ sometimes ❏ never	**If I see two students fighting in the playground I step in between them and tell them to stop.** ❏ always ❏ sometimes ❏ never
If my teacher dislikes me and punishes me for things I haven't done I report it to my parents and the principal. ❏ always ❏ sometimes ❏ never	**If I see a bigger student breaking the rules in the playground I tell them to stop.** ❏ always ❏ sometimes ❏ never

Positive Reinforcement: Activities and Strategies for Creating Confident Learners ISBN 978-1845901417 © 2010 Peter Clutterbuck

TRUSTING OTHERS

Students must learn that if they are told something personal and asked never to divulge it they must abide by this. Not doing so leads to a feeling of mistrust.

- Begin the lesson by telling the children something personal that others do not know. For example, "When I was 16 I wanted to become a nurse, but changed my mind and became a teacher."

- Now invite the children to divulge something about themselves that others do not know.

- Have the students discuss what the following statement means:

  "When you tell another a secret it is no longer a secret."

- Ask the children if they have ever told someone a secret they know about another person. If someone told them a secret about themselves would they keep it?

- Have children consider if it is fair or wise to reveal secrets you have been told. Would good friends do this?

- What is meant by the word *gossip*?

- A person once said: "If they are gossiping about me at least they are leaving someone else alone." Do the students agree?

- Have children discuss the saying:

  "Only a friend can betray you."

- Ask the students to think about a time they may have told someone something in confidence only to find they have told lots of other people. How did this make them feel?

Name ....

Date ....

TRUSTING OTHERS

Trust and loyalty are important values that we should always abide by. If you give your word – keep it.

■ In Box A write two things a person can do to show loyalty to friends.

■ In Box B write two ways we could demonstrate we are loyal to our parents.

■ In Box C write two ways we could demonstrate our loyalty to our school.

■ In Box D write two ways we could demonstrate our loyalty to our country.

A. ....

B. ....

C. ....

D. ....

Positive Reinforcement: Activities and Strategies for Creating Confident Learners ISBN 978-184590141-7 © 2010 Peter Clutterbuck

More Activities and Ideas for Interpersonal Development

The following activities can help to improve students' interpersonal skills.

MY GRADE

Have the students write a passage describing what they think are the best features of their class.

SURVEY

Ask the students questions about their school or class. The students can give a written response of Always, Sometimes or Never (this also enables teachers to determine the feelings certain students may have about their classmates).

Questions should include:

■ Do the students in this class care for each other?

■ Do the students in this class support each other in the playground?

■ Do you feel safe and welcome in this class?

PROUD BOARD

Have students work in small groups constructing a mural which illustrates things the people in their group are proud of.

WE CAN MAKE A DIFFERENCE

Have students break up into small groups and discuss ways they can help others. Each group may wish to develop a project to carry out their plans (e.g. chatting to the elderly in retirement homes, volunteering for a local charity).

NAMES FOR SPELLING

Students will always be more friendly if they are called by their correct names. During the first weeks of school use the students' first and last names as part of a spelling programme.

LAUGHTER

Ask all students to close their eyes and relax. When they appear to be completely relaxed ask everybody to start laughing as loud as they can (you must also laugh out loud, of course). Soon they will all join in and the laughter will become contagious, natural and spontaneous. The students love it!

SMILE A WHILE

If there ever appears to be a great deal of tension or anxiety within the classroom defuse the situation by calling for a "smile break": "Righto let's take thirty seconds for a smile break – any volunteers for a smile?" Not only does this activity help to reduce anxiety, it also creates feelings of warmth and understanding amongst the children.

COOPERATIVE ACTIVITIES

These tasks can assist students in building rapport with each other and discovering what they may have in common:

- Creating a group wall mural on a theme.

- Solving logical thinking problems in small groups.

- Role-playing nursery rhymes etc. in small groups.

- Sharing the colouring of a complex, intricate drawing.

- Preparing and performing a funny skit or short play.

- Surveying others – eye colour, favourite foods, favourite sports, etc.

- Group research projects.

BEST OF THE BEST

Students divide themselves into small groups. Their job is to come to a decision through consensus on the best of the best in certain categories (e.g. the best pet, the best football team, the best rock group, the best place for a holiday, the best book in the classroom, the best age to be). They must present their work to the rest of the class.

FIXING THE EARTH

Students in small groups must decide what is the greatest problem facing the earth at the moment and how they would go about solving it (e.g. global warming, pollution, obesity, starvation, crime, war). Each group must decide on the greatest problem then work on ways to solve it. They must present their work to the rest of the class.

GOING FISHING

In small groups students must decide in order of importance what to take on a fishing trip. They number the items 1 to 10 (with 1 being the most important and 10 being the least important). When they have decided they must be able to justify their choices to the rest of the class.

1. Sunscreen
2. Lollies
3. Fishing rods
4. Frying pan
5. Tent
6. Soft drinks
7. Bait
8. Hats
9. Stove
10. First aid kit

HAPPY HOLIDAYS

Have the students break up into small groups. Tell them they recently pooled their pocket money and bought a ticket in a holiday competition, which they won. They can only go to one destination. Their job as a group is to decide by consensus which one they will choose:

- Gold Coast (Australia)

- London (UK)

- Disneyland (USA)

- Beijing (China)

- Grand Canyon (USA)

- Kenya (African wildlife safari)

- Egypt (the Great Pyramids)

- Tokyo (Japan)

FIRE

A fire is headed for the home in which you and your three pals are playing. You only have time to take one thing each with you when you are rescued. Which four things would your group decide to take? You must all fully agree on the four things chosen:

■ Collection of family photos.

■ A wad of £50 notes.

■ Your best clothes.

■ Passports and birth certificates.

■ A famous painting.

■ Your mother's jewellery.

■ The DVD player.

■ Your old dog.

■ An old family heirloom.

■ A grandfather clock.

CLASSROOM QUESTIONNAIRE

Finding Your Twin

Ask students to find someone in the class who is the same as they are in the following ways. They can only write the same person's name twice.

Find Someone Who –

1. Follows the same football team as you do ....

2. Name begins with the same letter as yours does ....

3. Has the same favourite food as you do ....

4. Has a birthday in the same month as you do ....

5. Has the same colour eyes as you do ....

6. Has the same number of brothers and sisters as you do ....

7. Has the same favourite colour as you do ....

8. Has the same favourite TV show as you have ....

9. Has the same middle name as you have ....

10. Has the same favourite hobby as you have ....

11. Has the same favourite fast food as you do ....

12. Has the same favourite sport as you do ....

13. Has a parent who has the same first name as yours does ....

14. Has parents who drive the same make of car yours do ....

15. Who has been with you in the same class since you began school ....

(Note: Students can sign their name in the space if desired.)

An alternate research project is to try to fit someone into each description given below. Students must try to find a different person for each line. Students may write a name or get the students who fit that category to sign in the spaces.

Find Someone Who –

1. Has been overseas.

2. Has broken an arm or leg.

3. Has had a stay in hospital.

4. Has had a tooth pulled out by a dentist.

5. Has a guinea pig for a pet.

6. Was born in the same month as you.

7. Has been captain of a sporting team.

8. Has been at this school all their school life.

9. Has the same zodiac sign as you.

10. Has a brother or sister going to this school.

11. Rides a bicycle to school.

12. Has been at this school for less than two years.

13. Has ridden a horse.

14. Has been stung by a bee or wasp.

15. At least one parent comes from overseas.

The Friendly Classroom

SOME IDEAS FOR TEACHERS

In a friendly classroom all students enjoy helping with classroom chores. By doing so they become more responsible, more capable and feel part of the classroom team. At the same time you can build a team spirit and a sense of belonging.

Discuss with students early in the year the kinds of jobs that need to be done in a classroom. List as many of these as you can think of, then decide which ones should be assigned each week and which ones should be up for grabs.

Encourage students to choose their own jobs or chores. In this way they are less likely to complain about doing them and if they are doing the chore they have chosen they will feel much more responsible. Try switching classroom chores every week. This will provide an opportunity for each student to experience a variety of jobs. For the shy, timid student being given a difficult job and encouraged will build self-esteem. Remember, doing a hard job well is very satisfying.

Set students up for success by teaching the skills for doing the job well. In some cases you can do the job with the student or get the previous student who did it successfully to teach the new student.

Always show appreciation and thank each monitor at the end of the week for a job well done.

Classroom jobs can be good fun and lead to a sense of belonging by doing special things together. For example, challenge students to organise special days or small fundraisers for a worthy charity.

Maintain a "Classroom Chores" chart which will remind students of their responsibilities. Use colourful or humorous ticks or stickers to decorate it.

Present the following statement to the students and ask them what its implications are for all class members:

'Remember there is no I in the word TEAM!'

Recommended Reading

Beere, J. (2010). *The Primary Learner's Toolkit*. Crown House Publishing, Carmarthen.

Bowkett, et al. (2010). *A Moon on Water*. Crown House Publishing, Carmarthen.

Clutterbuck, P. (2008). *Values*. Crown House Publishing, Carmarthen.

Duckworth, J. (2009). *The Little Book of Values*. Crown House Publishing, Carmarthen.

Greef, A. (2005). *Resilience: Personal skills for effective learning*. Crown House Publishing, Carmarthen.

Greef, A. (2005). *Resilience: Social skills for effective learning*. Crown House Publishing, Carmarthen.

Petersen, L. K. (2007). *Positively Me*. Brilliant Publications, Dunstable.

White, M. (2008). *Magic Circles*. Sage Publications, London.